Henry St. John, Viscount Bolingbroke

Twayne's English Authors Series

Bertram H. Davis, Editor

Florida State University

TEAS 362

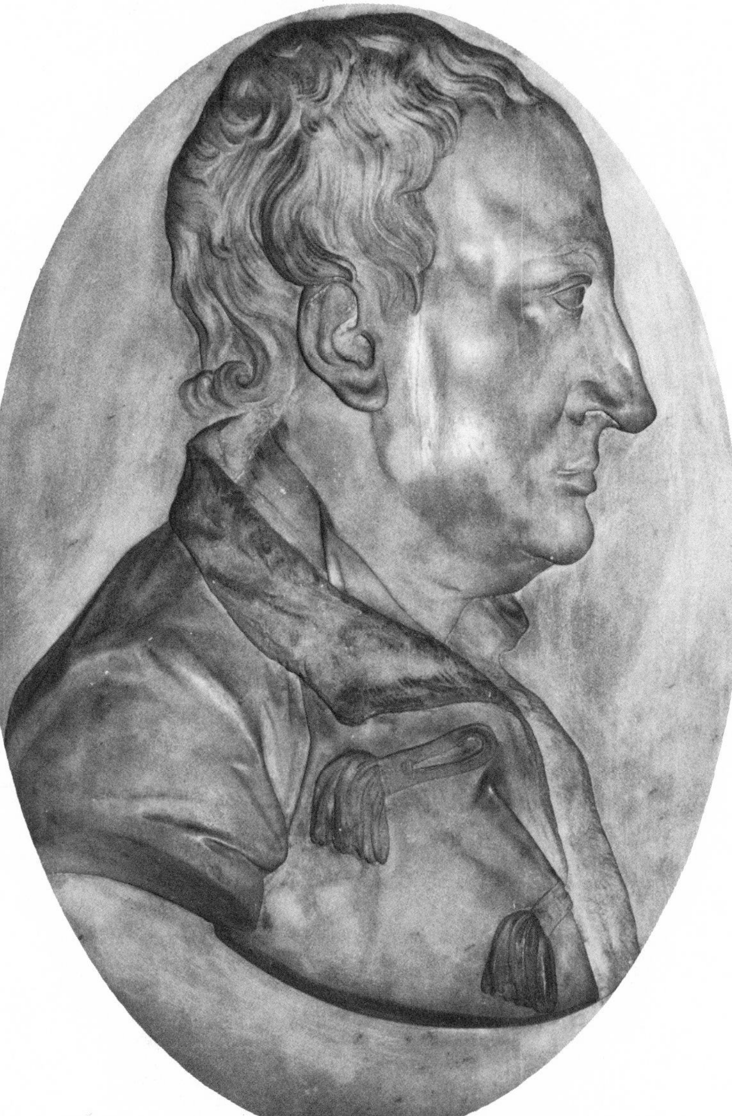

LORD BOLINGBROKE

(1678–1751)

Medallion portrait by Louis François Roubiliac
From the monument at St. Mary's Church, Battersea
Photography copyright © Simon Varey

Henry St. John, Viscount Bolingbroke

By Simon Varey

University of Utrecht

Twayne Publishers • Boston

Henry St. John,
Viscount Bolingbroke

Simon Varey

Published by Twayne Publishers
A Division of G. K. Hall & Company
70 Lincoln Street
Boston, Massachusetts 02111

Book Production by Marne B. Sultz

Book Design by Barbara Anderson

Printed on permanent/durable acid-free
paper and bound in the United States of
America.

Library of Congress Cataloging in Publication Data

Varey, Simon, 1951–
Henry St. John, Viscount Bolingbroke.

(Twayne's English authors series; TEAS 362)
Bibliography: p. 129
Includes index.
1. Bolingbroke, Henry St. John, Viscount, 1678–1751.
2. Politicians—Great Britain—Biography. I. Title.
II. Title: Henry Saint John, Viscount Bolingbroke.
III. Series.
DA501.B6V37 1984 941.07′092′4 [B] 83–22831
ISBN 0–8057–6848–3

For Christopher Macgregor

Contents

About the Author
Preface
Chronology

Chapter One
Bolingbroke's Career 1

Chapter Two
Bolingbroke and Rhetoric 15

Chapter Three
Early Writings 20

Chapter Four
The Politics of Liberty 34

Chapter Five
History and Patriotism 78

Chapter Six
The Philosophical Works 102

Chapter Seven
Bolingbroke and His Literary Milieu 112

Notes and References 119
Selected Bibliography 129
Index 135

About the Author

Simon Varey was born in London, England, and was educated at the University of Cambridge, where he took his M.A. and his Ph.D. in English Literature. In 1976 he left England to take up his present position as a lecturer in English at the University of Utrecht, the Netherlands. He has recently edited Bolingbroke's *Contributions to the "Craftsman,"* published by the Clarendon Press, and he has published articles on Bolingbroke, Pope, Gay, and the *Craftsman.* He is currently working on Fielding and neo-Palladian architecture.

Preface

Hailed as a genius, reviled as a traitor, renowned as a political journalist and historian, notorious as an atheist, celebrated as the friend and mentor of Pope and Swift, Lord Bolingbroke is—to say the least—colorful. He has attracted no fewer than thirteen full-length biographies, as well as many shorter studies, many of them inaccurate Tory *apologiae* for an apostle. But who reads Bolingbroke's voluminous work? The answer, apparently, is: political scientists and historians. One political scientist, Isaac Kramnick, has written the only good study of Bolingbroke's political ideology. And one historian, H. T. Dickinson, has written the only good biography and assessment of Bolingbroke's career. Indeed, until these two recent studies, Bolingbroke was thought to have displayed no consistent ideology in a career whose every action was thought to be motivated by opportunism.

Although many people read a little of Bolingbroke's output, few seem to survive the unattractive close print of four weighty volumes. In literary studies Bolingbroke still suffers from a strange semi-neglect as a figure known to be important but usually left to the historians. This is a pity, for Bolingbroke is a prose stylist who uses the English language skillfully, sometimes only to suit the needs of the moment, but more often to try to persuade his reader to share a coherent vision of Britain in a condition of dangerous decline. Bolingbroke is a considerable rhetorician, and it is through his rhetoric that I have approached his writings. An understanding of Bolingbroke as a rhetorician, and not solely as a philosopher or as an historian, places him in an important position in Augustan literature.

I have not discussed every work that Bolingbroke wrote, omitting altogether his least distinguished occasional tracts. I have devoted little space to his lengthy philosophical writings, which, though sometimes interesting, are disorganized and prolix. I have concentrated, instead, on Bolingbroke's political and historical writings, largely following the chronology of their publication.

The edition of Bolingbroke's writings used throughout is *The Works of Lord Bolingbroke*, 4 vols. (London, 1844; reprinted by Messrs. Frank Cass & Co. Ltd., 1967). When citing works not included in this collection, I have normally used first editions; but I refer the reader to my notes early in each chapter or section for enlightenment on parenthetical page references.

During Bolingbroke's lifetime Britain used the "Old Style" dating of the Julian calendar, but other western European nations used the "New Style" of the Gregorian calendar, whose dates were eleven days later. In this book, all dates are "Old Style" unless designated "N.S." The new year, however, is taken to begin on 1 January, not on 25 March.

The kindness of many people has helped me to write this book. The staffs of the British Library and Cambridge University Library have been courteous and helpful. To the former I am also grateful for permission to draw upon manuscripts in their possession. I am happy to thank the Marquess of Cholmondeley again for permission to use the Walpole papers, on deposit at Cambridge. I was also able to benefit from an all-too-brief visit to the Henry E. Huntington Library, San Marino, California. I am most grateful to H. T. Dickinson for permission to quote from his splendid *Bolingbroke* (1970). My warm thanks go to Greg Clingham, Maidie Collins, Howard Erskine-Hill, Maynard Mack, and Carol Varey, who have allowed me to benefit from their conversation, suggestions, time, and encouragement; and to Chris Coffin, who has been most hospitable. Michael Routh, who generously arranged his schedule to suit mine, heroically read a draft of the whole messy manuscript at a time when he had better things to occupy him, and he has made so many valuable suggestions that I can hardly thank him enough: he deserves better. I claim the mistakes as my own.

Simon Varey

University of Utrecht

Chronology

1678 Henry St. John born (16 September), probably at Lydiard Tregoze, Wiltshire, to Henry St. John, Sr., and Mary Rich, who dies within a fortnight.

1685 Accession of James II.

1687 Henry St. John, Sr., remarries.

1688 Protestant revolution: accession of William III.

1698 Henry St. John, Jr., begins a two-year tour, visiting France, Italy, and Switzerland.

1701 Becomes member of Parliament for Wootton Bassett, Wiltshire. Marries Frances Winchcombe.

1702 Receives an honorary degree from Christ Church, Oxford.

1704 Appointed Secretary at War, cementing connections with Robert Harley and the Duke of Marlborough.

1708 Resigns from office, and in the general election loses his seat in the Commons. During the parliamentary session, retires to Bucklebury, his wife's estate in Berkshire.

1710 Tories win general election. St. John appointed Secretary of State for the Northern Department in Harley's government. The *Examiner* launched (August); St. John writes *A Letter to the Examiner* and some unidentified contributions. Meets Jonathan Swift (November).

1712 Created Viscount Bolingbroke.

1713 The Treaty of Utrecht ends the War of the Spanish Succession. Swift publishes *The Conduct of the Allies.*

1714 Death of Queen Anne; accession of George I.

1715 Bolingbroke flees to France, is impeached in his absence for high treason, and enters the service of James Edward Stuart, as his Secretary of State. The Pretender's rebellion fails dismally.

1716 Dismissed by James. Writes *Reflections upon Exile.*

1717 Writes *A Letter to Sir William Windham*, which he soon circulates among leading Tories.

1718 Frances Winchcombe dies.

1719 Bolingbroke marries Marie-Claire de Marcilly, Marquise de Villette. They move to La Source, near Orléans. In France, Bolingbroke meets the Abbé Alary, the Marquis d'Argenson, and Voltaire.

1720 Financial collapse of the South Sea Company.

1722 Robert Walpole becomes principal minister.

1723 Bolingbroke receives royal pardon (April).

1724 Writes *Reflections concerning Innate Moral Principles.*

1725 Returns from exile, settling at Dawley Farm, near Uxbridge. Joins forces with William Pulteney and Sir William Wyndham to organize opposition to Walpole's government.

1726 Swift publishes *Gulliver's Travels* (October). Bolingbroke and Pulteney launch the *Craftsman* (December).

1727 Death of George I; accession of George II. Bolingbroke writes *The Occasional Writer*, nos. 1 to 3 (January-March).

1728 John Gay, *The Beggar's Opera* (January); Alexander Pope, *The Dunciad* (May).

1730–1731 Bolingbroke's *Remarks on the History of England* published serially in the *Craftsman.*

1733 The Excise crisis. Bolingbroke begins *A Dissertation upon Parties*, published serially in the *Craftsman.* Pope publishes the first three epistles of *An Essay on Man*, addressed to Bolingbroke.

1735 Bolingbroke leaves England for Argeville, in northern France. Writes *Letters on the Study and Use of History.*

1736 Moves to Chanteloup; writes his last four essays for the *Craftsman* and begins the *Letter on the Spirit of Patriotism.*

1737 Pope publishes the *Epistle to Augustus.* Death of Queen Caroline.

1738 Visiting Pope at Twickenham, Bolingbroke gives him

the manuscript of *Letters on the Study and Use of History*, for Pope to have it privately printed.

1739 England declares war on Spain (the "War of Jenkins' Ear").

1740 *The Idea of a Patriot King*, written in 1739, printed privately by Pope. Death of Sir William Wyndham.

1742 Walpole falls from power. Pope writes the *New Dunciad.*

1743 Pulteney created Earl of Bath. *Remarks on the History of England* published separately. *The Dunciad in Four Books* published.

1744 Death of Pope. Bolingbroke and his wife return to England, settling at Battersea.

1745 Deaths of Swift and Walpole. Jacobite rising of the Young Pretender.

1749 Bolingbroke publishes the "authorized" edition of the *Letters, on the Spirit of Patriotism, on the Idea of a Patriot King, and on the State of Parties at the Accession of King George I.*

1750 Death of Marie-Claire de Marcilly.

1751 Death of Bolingbroke (12 December). Buried alongside his wife, at St. Mary's Church, Battersea.

1752 *Letters on the Study and Use of History* published, causing immediate and considerable controversy. *Reflections concerning Innate Moral Principles* published for the first time.

1753 *A Letter to Sir William Windham, Some Reflections on the Present State of the Nation,* and *A Letter to Mr. Pope* published.

1754 David Mallet publishes his edition of Bolingbroke's *Works* in five volumes. The previously unpublished writings provoke an instant and hostile reaction.

1756 Edmund Burke parodies Bolingbroke in *The Vindication of Natural Society.*

Chapter One

Bolingbroke's Career

The Making of a Politician

Jonathan Swift wrote in his *Journal to Stella* on 23 February 1712 that "The Secrty [of State] is much the greatest Commoner in Engld, and turns the whole Parlmt, who can do nothing without him, and if he lives & has his health, will I believe be one day at the Head of Affairs. I have told him sometimes, that if I were a dozen years younger, I would cultivate his Favor, and trust my Fortune with his."[1] Swift was not alone in his admiration of the Secretary of State, Henry St. John, who was to become Viscount Bolingbroke later that year. John Gay called him "the most accomplish'd of his species"[2] and Alexander Pope told the Earl of Burlington on 19 December 1738 that Bolingbroke was "the Greatest Man I know, ever knew, or shall know."[3] Yet, despite this sort of admiration, Bolingbroke was widely viewed with suspicion by contemporaries who observed his fierce political ambition combined with a distinctly unstable temperament. This combination in fact denied Swift's prophecy: Bolingbroke did live and have his health until a painful cancer killed him in 1751, but he was never "at the Head of Affairs."

Bolingbroke pursued two political careers, one inside, one outside Parliament, and when the second failed like the first to bring him the results he wanted, he began a third career. Henry St. John's first career began with his entry into politics in February 1701, when at the age of twenty-two he became the member of Parliament for the family seat at Wootton Bassett. Of his life before this date, little is certain. It is known that he was brought up in a household that was far from stable, that he was probably educated at a dissenting academy (not, as was once thought, at Eton), and that he went on a Grand Tour between 1698 and 1700, visiting France, Italy, and Switzerland.[4]

St. John began quickly to make a name for himself in Parliament, where he aligned himself with the Tory party, in particular with its high church wing. Prompted by personal ambition as much as anything, he made a nuisance of himself by backing two extreme measures but taking care to show his own party, as well as the opposition Whigs, that he could be a dangerous opponent if he chose and that he might be worth buying off. But to make himself acceptable to the more moderate ministry and thereby gain a government post, St. John needed to embrace more moderate policies than those of the high church extremists. He therefore chose to dissociate himself from this extreme element and drift toward the moderate Robert Harley, with whom he was soon to be in close contact. St. John's policy paid off, for in April 1704 he moved into the ministry with the junior post of Secretary at War. Thus, in only three years, "he had won a reputation with the whole House of Commons, not merely with the less talented Tory backbenchers."[5] St. John's rise to political prominence was rapid, yet seemingly deserved: he had shown his capabilities, not the least important of which was his forceful and persuasive oratory.

But St. John had also been acquiring another, less savory reputation, for sexual licentiousness. It seems that he was more than a routine rake: he wanted to excel—and be known to excel—at everything he did, sex included. This attitude led to his disgraceful treatment of his first wife, Frances Winchcombe. Theirs was virtually a marriage of convenience, but this cannot excuse his neglect of her. Numerous anecdotes (mostly well founded) testify to his almost complete lack of care or interest in his wife during their seventeen years of marriage.[6] This early reputation for immorality, along with accusations of vanity and the criticism that he had wasted his talents, reappeared in St. John's public career when it suited his enemies.

As Secretary at War in the administration of the earl of Godolphin and the duke of Marlborough, St. John soon found that he had estranged himself from many of the Tories, not only from the extremists whom he had intentionally abandoned.[7] However, St. John's interest never lay with the Whigs, nor were the Whigs ever very sympathetic to him. Both St. John and Harley eventually resigned, in 1708, from the mixed administration after continued pressure from the Whigs, who wanted some return for their support in the House of Commons. Before his resignation, St. John had taken the precaution of renewing contact with those Tory leaders whom he had previously been content to ignore; but St. John was by no means obliged to resign. He meant what he said when he told Harley, "I am as much convinced as it is possible to be that going out of employment at the time and in the manner we did was equally honest and prudent. No man's opinion can add any weight to confirm me in this thought."[8] In these early years St. John was ambitious but not unscrupulous in his public life, yet until recently his critics and biographers preferred to think of him as an unprincipled opportunist.[9]

St. John's conduct during his four years at the War Office reveals other characteristics: relish of hard work, efficiency, willingness to pick up cash for himself in somewhat dubious ways, and a continuing drive for political power. He also acquired valuable experience of military administration at a time when England was at war with France, he established contact with the influential duke of Marlborough, whom he regarded (at first) as a hero, and he learned how to extend the political power of his post. But St. John's ambitious desire suffered a setback when he lost his Commons seat in the general election of May 1708 and could find no other seat. He was therefore obliged to sit out the next parliament, leading the life of a country gentleman at Bucklebury (his wife's country estate in Berkshire), and although he professed to enjoy this retired life, he was impatient to be back in the active political world, where now the Whigs once more held control of government.

This failure to be reelected in 1708 caused St. John to damage the intimacy of his relationship with Harley, whom he held, along with other Tories, partly responsible for his defeat.[10] Yet he was ready to approve Harley's tactics of intrigue during 1710, which exploited weaknesses in the Whig administration and sought to broaden the appeal of his own moderation. Harley was instrumental in destroying Godolphin's ministry, but he wanted power in his own hands, not in those of the Tory party, nor in those of pushing, ambitious men like St. John, whom he was particularly reluctant to include in his cabinet.[11] But St. John pestered for a senior post, and finally got one when Harley made him Secretary of State for the Northern Department. Harley, for all his caution, had now got St. John beside him once again, and before long "the captain" would be bidding for "the colonel's" leadership.

St. John and Harley worked together in relative harmony during 1710, and although St. John was beginning to question some of Harley's policies, both men agreed on the importance of ending the war with France. Despite Marlborough's spectacular military successes, the war had dragged on for too long and was proving expensive. For St. John there was the additional point that its expenses were, by means of the land tax, impoverishing the landed gentry, for whose cause he retained a good deal of sympathy throughout his life.

Gradually the friendship between Harley and St. John deteriorated, and matters between them came to a head for the first time in March 1711 when Antoine de Guiscard, a Frenchman being examined for treason, made an attempt on Harley's life.[12] Seriously wounded, Harley could not perform his duties for some months. St. John tried to capitalize on Harley's absence, first claiming that he himself had been the real target of Guiscard's knife. St. John also discovered that he had been deliberately excluded from knowledge of preliminary peace negotiations with France[13]—further evidence that Harley did not trust him.

With Harley away, St. John tried to take control of both the ministry and the Tory party, but he could not win the trust of the House of Commons, where he lacked Harley's sure touch, and in the cabinet he committed a number of blunders. To make matters worse, Harley had gained considerable public sympathy after the assassination attempt, so that his return was marked by increased popularity. St. John was jealous and disappointed, but his ambitious spirit was indomitable. The friendship between the two men had been breached, by these incidents and by St. John's conduct in the cabinet and the Commons in January and February 1711: St. John had tried to force through the cabinet a proposal to capture Quebec, but only Harley's enforced absence allowed St. John to have his way; in the Commons St. John was more than likely behind the anti-ministry tactics of "a formidable pressure-group of Tory backbenchers, the October Club."[14] The breach widened still further, until in mid-1713 it became an open war. Even in July 1712, when St. John was created Viscount Bolingbroke, he considered his elevation not an honor but a slight. "I was," he said, "dragged into the house of lords in such a manner, as to make my promotion a punishment, not a reward":[15] he had wanted and expected an earldom. In St. John's eyes, Harley, who had been created earl of Oxford, had got the better of him.

During these years, both Harley and St. John recognized the value of the press as a political weapon.[16] Their principal vehicle of propaganda was the weekly *Examiner*, whose editorship was soon entrusted to Harley's friend Jonathan Swift. Apart from writing the paper's statement of policy, *A Letter to the Examiner*, St. John also contributed essays to its early issues. His contribution to the press was great. The *Craftsman*, which he founded with William Pulteney in 1726, enlivened political writing for the ten years he was involved with it, and the status of journalism itself was raised by the participation of one so eminent. When he and his fellow contributors complained in the late 1720s of illegal restraints on the press, Bolingbroke was often reminded that he had prosecuted many writers and printers during his time as Secretary of State: he had been unstinting, but not really successful, in such prosecutions.

Swift was entrusted from November 1710 with the task of justifying the largely Tory ministry in the press. That St. John and Harley believed that propaganda could be effective is demonstrated both by the conduct of the paper war in 1710–11 and by the composition of the most famous of pamphlets, Swift's *Conduct of the Allies* (1711).[17] The preliminary peace negotiations, upon which St. John was striving to place his personal stamp, had brought Britain little real gain by late 1711, but the *Conduct of the Allies* sought to defend the negotiations by accusing Britain's allies of evading their responsibilities and neglecting British interests. Furthermore, Swift, surely responding to St. John's view, linked "the unjustified complaints of the allies with the factious opposition of the Whigs,"[18] and transformed "stale protests about Dutch inadequacies and sporadic snipings at Marlborough into a massive indictment of the war."[19]

The War of the Spanish Succession was brought to a long-awaited formal conclusion with the Treaty of Utrecht in 1713. This settlement was, in Isaac Kramnick's words, "Bolingbroke's great achievement in these years,"[20] and Bolingbroke spoke of it with pride in years to come, but the extent of Oxford's involvement was actually greater than it seemed and greater than Bolingbroke's, and several elements in the final proposals were rejected by Parliament, to Bolingbroke's chagrin. However, the treaty was popular, both in and out of Parliament, and with Oxford finding it increasingly difficult to keep his rival at bay, Bolingbroke made his second, serious bid for the leadership in the summer of 1713. His attempt was probably doomed by his inability ever to gain the confidence of Queen Anne, who held Oxford in high regard. But during 1713 the queen began to grow dissatisfied with Oxford, who, astonishingly, was neglecting to attend her: this was the main reason for Bolingbroke's "imperious language and growing confidence."[21] Further, although the Tory party had increased its majority in the 1713 general election, there was no unity within its ranks. To gain sufficient support to challenge Oxford, it was important for Bolingbroke to win converts from different sectors of the party, but more important to win the queen's favor, so he did his best to cultivate influential members of her court, most notably

Lady Masham. She and Bolingbroke finally persuaded the queen to dismiss Oxford, but Anne did not promote Bolingbroke to the Lord Treasurership. Worse still, she almost immediately fell mortally ill. Instead of adhering to his earlier plan of trying to unite the Tories, Bolingbroke lost his judgment and foolishly tried to arrange a deal with several prominent Whigs.

The queen's illness, and her death on 1 August 1714, threw into the forefront of public affairs the most delicate and harassing problem of her reign, the succession. The Tory party had been sufficiently disunited to include voluble elements of support for a Hanoverian monarch to succeed Anne, side by side with many who sympathized with the cause of the Pretender, James Edward Stuart. Among James's supporters, privately, was Bolingbroke, who had been in communication with the Pretender, and who was at once suspected of treason when the Whigs took power in 1714. The Hanoverian Succession had been assured (in the event of Anne's dying without an heir, as she did) by the Act of Settlement (1701), but there were still many adherents to the Pretender's cause, most of them Tories. When the Elector of Hanover became King George I in August 1714, the Whigs who had long courted him and had in effect brought him to England were back in control. George, predictably, had little sympathy with Jacobites, and despite token attempts by the late Tory ministry to pay court to him in Hanover, he had little time for either Oxford or Bolingbroke. Bolingbroke still believed early in 1715 that a united Tory party could govern with George's assent, but his own relations with Oxford had helped to destroy the Tory party as a coherent force. Once the Whigs had taken over, Bolingbroke's future looked bleak, and when the new ministry ordered the seizure of papers of various members of the outgoing government, gossip and rumor reached his ears, informing him that he might be convicted of Jacobitism. Bolingbroke chose to flee to France and escaped arrest by a few hours.

Exile

Bolingbroke's parliamentary career came to an abrupt end in March 1715. Throughout this career he had shown that his political sympathies lay with the Tory "squirearchy" but as yet his career had been founded on little more than ambition: he had scarcely articulated his political principles. His image as a mere adventurer was emphasized by his flight. Having insisted on his loyalty to the Hanoverian Succession to a company of leading Whigs, Bolingbroke laid himself open to a charge of hypocrisy by running away: the new ministry took this as confirmation of his guilt and initiated proceedings, in his absence, to impeach him. One month after the announcement of his impeachment in the Commons, Bolingbroke accepted an earldom from the Pretender and became his Secretary of State. He was never allowed to forget that this decision was the worst blunder of his entire career, compounded in 1733 by his acceptance of a pension from the French court.

For the rest of his life Bolingbroke had to become used to being called a traitor: after such transparently self-serving behavior, he enjoyed little public confidence. Afterwards, he could do no more than attempt to justify his loyalty to the Pretender, who proved to be intractable and incompetent. When the Pretender planned his attempt to usurp the crown in 1715, Bolingbroke saw that it would fail and said so, but his advice was not heeded and James dismissed him. Bolingbroke insisted that his dismissal was a sign that his attachment to the whole Jacobite cause was permanently broken.[22]

After his dismissal in March 1716, Bolingbroke set about the long process of trying to reinstate himself in England. He curried favor with King George and the more moderate Whigs by offering privately to reveal information about James and his supporters. At the same time, with Jacobite propaganda to vilify him now in circulation, he needed to ensure that he did not alienate his former Tory colleagues, whom he was determined not to betray. It was from this period that Bolingbroke's task of reviving and reuniting the Tory party began, and the first step toward establishing his own credibility as a politician was to eradicate, or at least palliate, the stigma of Jacobitism. His second political career began to take shape as his task became the balancing act in which he tried to bring together Tories, dissident Whigs, and even some Jacobites, without presenting a program of Jacobitism. The result was to play down old Whig-Tory differences, still rife in the aftermath of the uprising, and to apologize for his own excesses by implying that they had been the product of party strife.[23] He continued to insist that party struggles and squabbles were a source of nothing but trouble, and recommended realistic government based on the moderate elements of both parties. The balance had been achieved once Bolingbroke ensured that he was not seen to be betraying his former Jacobite colleagues: his method was to circulate among his Tory friends his *tour de force* of self-justification,

A Letter to Sir William Windham, written in 1717. Wyndham was the virtual leader of the Tory opposition in the Commons, certainly the most prominent member of the party, and also an old friend of Bolingbroke, yet the letter was coolly received by the leading Tories who read it in 1718.

Bolingbroke's largely self-imposed exile lasted for ten years. His wife had died in October 1718, but for nearly two years he had been living with the brilliant Marie Claire de Marcilly. They married privately in 1719, publicly in 1722, and settled in 1720 at La Source, near Orléans.[24] During these years of retirement, Bolingbroke, preparing, as it happened, for his future writing, read widely in politics, philosophy, and history. Through his meeting numerous aristocrats and scholars, he came into "contact with ideas of people who were playing a crucial role in the development of the French Enlightenment."[25] These included Voltaire (who was most impressed by the English lord), Henri de Boulainvilliers, Lévesque de Pouilly (a disciple of Newton), and an English Newtonian, Brook Taylor. But perhaps the two most important contacts were those he made with René Louis de Voyer, the Marquis d'Argenson, and Pierre Joseph, the Abbé Alary. Alary, says Kramnick, "initiated Bolingbroke into the mysteries of historiography and the French school of scepticism and pyrronhism,"[26] but it is also true that the then little-known Abbé revered Bolingbroke as much as the latter respected him. Alary was the founder, and d'Argenson the historian, of the Club de l'Entresol, which Bolingbroke joined. From 1723 to 1731 the club met at weekends: one hour in each meeting was devoted to news in the press, in particular news of international affairs, and discussion would then move to European diplomacy.[27] Members of the club sometimes read papers: Bolingbroke wrote his *Reflections concerning Innate Moral Principles* for this purpose and read it to the club, perhaps in 1724.[28]

Meanwhile, Bolingbroke impatiently awaited his restoration, expecting his attainder to be reversed, but hating the disagreeable uncertainty.[29] After continually pestering the right influential people and giving a large bribe to the duchess of Kendal (one of George's mistresses), Bolingbroke received a royal pardon on 25 May 1723. There still remained the matter of his estates, which he had forfeited by his attainder, but which he naturally wanted back. Robert Walpole, now well established at the head of the Whig administration, and already one of Bolingbroke's bitter enemies, supported at the king's behest the restoration of Bolingbroke's estates in April 1725, even though he had opposed it violently twice before, in 1719 and 1721. The rivalry and hatred between these two men are well known. Two more emphatically dissimilar temperaments would be hard to find: the well-born Bolingbroke, witty, gay, brilliant, "mercurial" as he was known, but rash and apt to lose his nerve under pressure; and Walpole the uncouth plodder, diligent but reliable, sedulous but not gifted with his rival's quick wit. But Walpole was trusted by the king and many independents in Parliament; Bolingbroke was not. Despite support from the throne and Parliament, Walpole feared a Whig revolt over so politically sensitive an issue as the return of Bolingbroke's estates. At the same time, a Commons motion to permit Bolingbroke to regain his seat in the House of Lords was defeated: Walpole himself, opposing this motion, reminded the Whigs that Bolingbroke could not regain political power.

Opposition to Walpole

Upon his return to English politics, Bolingbroke at once endeavored to "supplant the minister by means of the royal mistresses,"[30] considering himself released from any honorable agreement because, he claimed, Walpole had broken a promise by refusing a full restoration. Bolingbroke's opposition to Walpole was immediately open and hostile. Until 1725, the Tory party in opposition had continued to be fragmented, disorganized, and ineffective. It was time for a suitable figure to espouse the cause of the discontented and endow it with some organization and sense of purpose, and it was in 1725, when Bolingbroke gave the opposition an organized program, that the Commons saw some combined resistance to the ministry. Also in 1725, William Pulteney fell from Walpole's favor "after several manifestations of mutual hostility"[31] and was dismissed from office. Pulteney at once joined the opposition, becoming the automatic leader by virtue of his superb oratorical skills. Sir William Wyndham became his able lieutenant. Bolingbroke's modern biographer, H. T. Dickinson notes that to "fuse the Tories into an organised, coherent group was a major task. . . . Men like William and Daniel Pulteney did not differ with Walpole on any question of principle. Their hostility was the product of frustrated ambition."[32] Although this may have been their initial motive, their opposition soon bore signs of both principle and policy. To have any chance of rebuilding his political career, Bolingbroke had to turn to dissident Whigs like the Pulteney cousins.

Between them they appealed to Whigs and Tories simultaneously, both inside and outside Parliament. The vehicle for their appeal was their new essay periodical, the *Craftsman.*

For a time, Bolingbroke seriously entertained hopes of a return to real political power. He tried first the conventional Hanoverian source of preferment, the Prince of Wales (who viewed him with some suspicion), and then struggled for elevation via the king's mistresses and the king himself, but he was discouraged. With all his immediate paths to power blocked, Bolingbroke turned again to political writing. For as long as the *Craftsman*, with its large circulation, continued to be read avidly, Bolingbroke probably retained some hope of political power, but, more important, he kept alive his hopes of national renovation.

The first essential step toward national improvement had to be the removal of Walpole and his system of "corruption." Pulteney apparently did not seek control of government,[33] but he felt he had a score to settle with Walpole and vowed to pursue him "to his *Destruction.*"[34] With the removal of the minister as their principal objective, the two strands of opposition could unite: at times this appeared to be their only aim.

The opposition enjoyed limited success. Walpole was finally removed, but his dismissal took longer to achieve than that of any other first minister in British history. The disparate principles behind the opposition were sufficiently incoherent—despite Bolingbroke's efforts to unite them—to render the whole program unworkable for any one administration, so that the opposition was "unlikely to carry Bolingbroke and Pulteney into office with a parliamentary majority behind them."[35] Parliament saw this, and Walpole was never, with the sole exception of the Excise crisis, seriously embarrassed. In his attempt to unite the opposition, Bolingbroke, in Dickinson's words,

> inspired the most important and fascinating opposition campaign of the eighteenth century. He fought Walpole on two levels. On the one hand he looked about him for any and every expedient and issue, real or imagined, which could be used to embarrass Walpole and weaken his hold on power. In this battle he himself fought through the press, but had to rely on his friends and allies in parliament to follow his advice. A much more significant contest was waged on a theoretical and philosophical level. In his search for a viable programme he eventually elaborated important ideas and concepts of opposition, which raised the whole level of the debate above the more obvious and very real contest for power.[36]

Both these levels constituted the platform on which the *Craftsman* was raised: the "theoretical and philosophical level" was as much a concern in the press as the more immediate, more superficial method of attacking Walpole.

During the campaign of opposition Bolingbroke lived at his "farm" at Dawley, paying and receiving visits within a most distinguished circle of acquaintance. Regular visitors included Dr. John Arbuthnot, Wyndham, Alexander Pope, the Pulteneys, John Gay, as well as other politicians and the *Craftsman*'s editor, Nicholas Amhurst. Swift, away from Dublin for the summer of 1726, stayed at Dawley. Many of the weekly *Craftsman* essays were composed at Dawley by members of Bolingbroke's circle.[37]

Bolingbroke himself found a valuable outlet for his energies in this extra-parliamentary career. His literary talent was considerable, and his decision to satirize Walpole's government in pamphlets and periodical essays long influenced the pattern of politics and political literature. At first, he evidently thought that the *Craftsman* alone was not enough, for in the first two months of 1727 he also wrote three substantial political pamphlets under the title of the *Occasional Writer*, to supplement early *Craftsman* essays. Beween 1728 and 1731, when the *Craftsman* was well established, Bolingbroke wrote further pamphlets on controversial issues, expressing himself at greater length than the confines of a short essay would permit.

Political journalism was not, however, his only literary activity. Between 1725 and 1735 he frequently enjoyed Pope's company, and the products of their many conversations, with a firm base in Bolingbroke's philosophical studies, were written and revised during the 1730s, to be published posthumously in 1754 as four letters to Pope. Also during the 1720s and 1730s, Bolingbroke's ideas and suggestions influenced Pope's poems, possibly Swift's *Gulliver's Travels*, and Gay's *Beggar's Opera* and second series of *Fables*.

Exile, again

Bolingbroke's involvement in his campaign to oust Walpole lasted until 1735, when a combination of events obliged him to withdraw. Walpole delivered a stinging speech in the Commons that shattered Bolingbroke's credibility and shamed a number of independent backbenchers into supporting the ministry rather than the old schemer.[38] Bolingbroke, possibly oversensitive, also detected hints that Walpole knew of his near-treasonable connection with the French court. Furthermore, Bolingbroke and Pulteney had become disenchanted with one another, and the Opposition Whigs were beginning to look on Bolingbroke as an expensive luxury. He gave up in June 1735, retiring to Chanteloup in northern France, from where he sent his last four *Craftsman* essays in March and April 1736.

In this new exile Bolingbroke began to return to his books. The first result was *Letters on the Study and Use of History*, in which he presented his view of the nature and usefulness of history, particularly as a moral and philosophical commentary on the present. The *Letters* also give some account of European diplomatic history from 1659 to 1713, including Bolingbroke's own conduct in the ministry. Although this was the first of his several publications of historical philosophy to be written after his departure from England, the *Letters* have an analogous source in his first two connected works of political philosophy, the *Remarks on the History of England* (1730–31) and *A Dissertation upon Parties* (1733–34), both first published serially in the *Craftsman.* In these works he had shown his belief in the value of history, and his own ability as a historiographer. The *Remarks*, using the history of England to throw Walpole into a most unfavorable light, had put into practice the theory that appeared later in the *Letters.* Most significantly, Bolingbroke had shown his skill as a political rhetorician.

Despite his retirement to France in 1735, Bolingbroke did not easily give up active participation in British politics. Over the next nine years his home was in France, in Argeville after a year at Chanteloup, but he paid regular visits to England for various reasons, such as supervising the sale of Dawley, arranging the details of the inheritance from his father (who died in 1742), and—most importantly—offering more political advice to the opposition. He also extended his 1744 visit in order to remain with Pope, who was dying. Late in 1744 Bolingbroke and his wife finally returned to England to live in his family home at Battersea, after nine years in which his extensive political experience had been in demand among the new members of the young "patriot" opposition, William Pitt, Lord Cobham, Lord Cornbury, George Lyttelton, and Lord Polwarth. Bolingbroke's *Letter on the Spirit of Patriotism*, addressed to Cornbury, suggested—as early as 1736—that a promising future could lie with a new generation of men of superior talents who had not grown up amid the fierce party rancor of the reigns of William III and Anne. The future certainly did not lie with Pulteney and his followers: Pulteney tamely capitulated in 1742, spending most of his energy seeking to be bought off, until his retirement to the Lords as earl of Bath in 1743. As the 1740s progressed, however, Bolingbroke's advice was heeded less and less, until he had become a kind of neglected consultant rather than the useful and experienced campaigner he thought he was. He was eventually ignored altogether.

Bolingbroke seems to have clung to an ever-diminishing hope of continued participation in the political world until the late 1740s. His best-known political treatise, *The Idea of a Patriot King* (written in late 1738 or early 1739), was ostensibly an attempt to solve all the problems that had faced him during his years of opposition. Bolingbroke also wrote *The State of Parties at the Accession of King George I*, probably in 1739: here he played down party distinctions once again and claimed some of the credit for suppressing them, but the real object of this pamphlet was to urge the young patriots to ignore party divisions.

Bolingbroke outlived most of his friends. Wyndham died in 1740, Pope in 1744, Swift in 1745, and Marie Claire in 1750. In each case Bolingbroke expressed profound grief that amounted to despair, but his estimate of his tender-hearted, valued friend Pope was revised when he learned in 1749 of Pope's surreptitious printing of the *Patriot King.* After resettling at Battersea in 1744, Bolingbroke lived out his last ten years as a rather lonely, embittered old man. The bright prospects of the ambitious days before 1710 had become only a brief spell of power and fame, shattered by his own temperament. He always liked power, or the prospect of it,[39] but during his first exile he had lived in perpetual frustration despite his protestations to the contrary, until the revival of his hopes with the campaign against Walpole. In the end even this optimism faded, and Bolingbroke was obliged finally to give up altogether when the death of the Prince of Wales early in 1751 destroyed what little remained of the old man's political hopes.

Few people loved Bolingbroke, and he loved few. He certainly cared little for his first wife, but he was devoted to his second. His loves were deep and loyal; he felt that his later attitude to Pope was justified on grounds of betrayed trust. Bolingbroke was a schemer, and as such could never win loyalty, but only a somewhat suspicious respect, from most who knew him. Yet the great literary men of the day almost worshipped him. His public career was always hampered by his inability to command the respect of Parliament, as Harley and Walpole commanded it, although neither was as accomplished an orator as he. Even after his death in December 1751 Bolingbroke's name was associated with dangerous tendencies, and his reputation was further vilified when the Scottish poet David Mallet published Bolingbroke's *Works* in 1754. Samuel Johnson's widely known judgment is still worth quoting: Bolingbroke "was a scoundrel, and a coward: a scoundrel, for charging a blunderbuss against religion and morality; a coward, because he had not resolution to fire it off himself, but left half a crown to a beggarly Scotchman, to draw the trigger after his death!"[40] Johnson had not read Bolingbroke's works. One typical response declared that "In sober religious Times, when Men are rather deeply sensible of their religious Duties, than clamorous about their religious Professions, the pretended Philosophy of Lord *Bolingbroke* will meet with a deserved Indignation and Contempt."[41] It was impossible to be neutral about Bolingbroke. Lord Chesterfield told his son that "Lord Bolingbroke joined all the politeness, the manners, and the graces of a courtier, to the solidity of a statesman, and to the learning of a pedant. He was *omnis homo*."[42] More simply, Chesterfield told the Marquise de Monconseil that Bolingbroke's death meant the loss of "a warm, kind, and instructive friend."[43]

Whatever Bolingbroke's gifts and achievements, few have agreed with Pope that Bolingbroke would "be the greatest man in the world, either in his own time, or with posterity."[44]

Chapter Two

Bolingbroke and Rhetoric

Despite many rescue attempts, rhetoric has on the whole had a bad reputation since Gorgias admitted, in the fifth century B.C., that a rhetorician need not concern himself with truth. In 1690 John Locke called rhetoric "that powerful instrument of error and deceit."[1] In a more recent view, "Rhetoric, as the Puritans well knew, is essentially a Machiavellian art—it deals primarily with what is effective and only secondarily with what is right."[2]

The generally unfavorable reputation of rhetoric does not, however, mean that all rhetoricians are disreputable, but only that rhetoric has fallen into disrepute by being abused. Like Aristotle, Bolingbroke and his friends distinguish true from false rhetoric. Swift recounts that lawyers misuse forensic rhetoric to argue that black is white,[3] and Pope claims that

> There foam'd rebellious *Logic*, gagg'd and bound,
> There, stript, fair *Rhet'ric* languish'd on the ground;
> His blunted Arms by *Sophistry* are born,
> And shameless *Billingsgate* her Robes adorn.[4]

Bolingbroke agrees with Swift and Pope that rhetoric in contemporary Britain has fallen into decay through misuse:

> Eloquence [or rhetoric] and History are God knows, at the lowest ebb imaginable among us. The different Stiles are not fix'd, the Bar and the Pulpit have no Standard, and our Historys are Gazettes ill digested, & worse writ. The case is far otherwise in France and in Italy. Eloquence has been extremely cultivated in both Countrys, . . .[5]

Thus Bolingbroke, before all other things an orator, sets out to restore rhetoric to a position of eminence by raising standards. For Bolingbroke, the decay of rhetoric, history, and poetry signifies the moral decay of the nation. To restore them is to help restore the nation's moral condition. With this aim in view, Bolingbroke and his friends adopt many techniques of classical rhetoric to express their deepest moral convictions.

Of the ancients, Quintilian and Aristotle affirmed that the orator, to be persuasive, must be and be seen to be virtuous. Their view returned to prominence in the eighteenth century in the earl of Shaftesbury's *Characteristics* (1711), but with a difference. In order to persuade a reader (the purpose of written rhetoric), the writer must give himself at least the *appearance* of virtue. The word *rhetoric* in the modern critical vocabulary often implies an author's strategy of presenting himself. In the context of the eighteenth century, this strategy usually encourages recognition of, say, Swift's "masks" or Pope's "poet in the poems."[6] To present oneself, or for that matter to seek to persuade anyone at all, presupposes an audience. The lawyer cannot plead without a court; the statesman cannot orate without a parliament; and the man of letters cannot write without a reader. To persuade these audiences, the lawyer, the statesman, and the writer must present themselves in the most appealing light. The rhetorical narrator must therefore *appear* at least to be virtuous in order to control his audience.

As a writer Bolingbroke found himself in a difficult position. He had a personal reputation for anything but virtue; and after his flight to France in 1715, his enemies condemned him as a traitor and dismissed anything he wrote as pernicious and untrustworthy. Bolingbroke's solution was to conceal his real self and to create another self in his writing, a persona who would be seen as being virtuous and moderate and who could thus more effectively persuade an audience. Because it suggests insincerity, Bolingbroke's rhetorical method of self-presentation, which diverts attention from the facts of his life and seeks to control his audience, is just the sort of device that gives rhetoric—and Bolingbroke himself—a bad name. Bolingbroke uses the device of the persona in works as various as *A Letter to Sir William Windham*, the *Letters on the Study and Use of History*, and even his philosophical writings, as well as in the most prominent and sustained case, the *Craftsman*. But although he was obliged, in these works, to adopt a rhetorical strategy that tended to conceal himself, such a technique, far from being dishonest, was necessary for a legitimate intellectual purpose. All Bolingbroke's rhetorical strategies were designed to persuade as wide a range of readers as possible, people pursuing different aims, values, and activities. The same strategies occur in Bolingbroke's political and nonpolitical writing, and even in his ostensibly private works.

Bolingbroke usually seeks to persuade his readers by means of logical argument rather than satiric fiction, using plain rather than figurative language, straightforward rather than convoluted syntax, common words rather than polysyllabic latinate ones. Whenever he writes about trade, his language is plain and his tone emphatic and assertive. "Trade," he insists typically in one *Craftsman* essay, "is of that general Use and Importance to every Country, that whatever relates to it, can never be unseasonable, nor too often discussed; especially in this Nation, which has so great a Dependance [*sic*] on it." He stresses that successful trade, manufacture, wealth, and strength are "the only Foundation of a *solid* and *lasting Greatness*."[7] In such essays, addressing London's merchants, Bolingbroke relies on a simple and direct appeal to their everyday experience. He appeals to the merchants' anger over Spanish piracy of their ships, in the expectation that he can bring to their attention the part Walpole plays in refusing to prevent the Spanish depredations. The plain style is designed to persuade the merchants to look beyond their own grievances and to accept the author's point that British traders suffer because trade has been weakened by the rise of the moneyed men. Arguing that self-interest and corruption motivate the moneyed men and therefore disadvantage the traders, and telling them that "a certain *great Man*" is ruining their prosperity, Bolingbroke clearly hopes to prompt the merchants to destroy corruption by removing Walpole.

The persuasive technique of most of Bolingbroke's writings makes use of irony, whether in such a simple reference as the "certain *great Man*" (aided by the emphasis of italic type) or in the subtler form of rhetorical questions. But of all Bolingbroke's rhetorical devices, one aroused the violent censure of his opponents: the ironic "example."

Bolingbroke uses the example, inherited from a Renaissance humanist tradition by way of the classics, to refer to and address a special class of persons: a king, a prince, or a statesman. But the example is also a rhetorical conception. The authors of the great Roman treatises on rhetoric held the example to be an effective means of instructing men in virtue and truth. Plutarch went further, saying that examples also stimulated morally virtuous conduct. Bolingbroke adopts this central idea from Roman rhetoric, that the example can teach and motivate men to virtue.[8] Remembering that the Romans thought that man could "improve" by contemplating heroic images, Bolingbroke depicts virtuous and vicious men as moral examples, in both his political and his apparently nonpolitical writing. Bolingbroke's use of the example does, for instance, suggest parallels between Walpole and some vicious men from history, but this device is also intended to encourage his readers to contemplate the virtuous so as to improve themselves, as a step toward removing moral corruption from public life. A humanist such as Bolingbroke, wishing to restore morality, needs to draw his values from history (as he does) and to communicate them to his public as convincingly as possible. Bolingbroke seeks to remove Walpole and to regain power, but his rhetoric is also directed to what he and his friends consider the renovation of a declining and corrupted nation.

Exemplary history, prominent in classical rhetoric, is also a technique favored by the Augustan satirists. Swift considers examples an "Expedient, frequently practised with great Safety and Success by satyrical Writers."[9] Reading history as a boy, Pope "would mark down: 'on such an occasion the people concerned proceeded in such a manner; it was evidently wrong and had a very ill effect; a statesman therefore should avoid it in a like case.' Such an one did very good or got an honest reputation by such an action: I would mark it down in order to imitate it where I had an opportunity."[10] These two comments, and Pope's defense of satire in a well-known letter to Arbuthnot, are quoted by Thomas Akstens, who shows that "By placing his argument for the cogency of example squarely in terms of the problem of virtue, Bolingbroke provides a link between the exemplar approach to history and the business of satire."[11] The example is a rhetorical weapon in the armory of satire. Because Bolingbroke demands that writing concerned with public life promote moral virtue, to him history and satire serve the same end.

The example occurs most commonly in Bolingbroke's apparently historical writing; indeed, it is the shaping force of his *Remarks on the History of England.* But that work is neither sober nor impartial history: it is satire. Echoing a passage from Bolingbroke's *Letters on the Study and Use of History*, Swift argues that satire has no place in historical writing. Scorning to fill his own *History of the Four Last Years of the Queen* with anything but truth, Swift says: "Neither shall I mingle Panegyrick or Satire with an History intended to inform Posterity, as well as to instruct those of the present Age, who may be Ignorant or Misled: Since Facts truly related are the best Applauses, or most lasting Reproaches."[12] Elsewhere Swift suggests that

There are two Ends that Men propose in writing Satyr; one of them less noble than the other, as regarding nothing further than the private Satisfaction, and Pleasure of the Writer; but without any View towards *personal Malice*: The other is a *publick Spirit,* prompting Men of *Genius* and Virtue, to mend the World as far as they are able. And as both these Ends are innocent, so the latter is highly commendable.[13]

Bolingbroke's association of his various personae with virtue and his stated aim of restoring or "mending" the political world suggest that his purpose accords with Swift's more "noble" type of satiric aim. Although not the same, satire and rhetoric are closely related, and frequently the borderline between them is not clear. Both activities are public, and in Bolingbroke's time both were frequently political as well. As Peter Dixon puts it, "The satirist, like the orator, is entering a protest in public, addressing an audience with a view to changing its attitudes and disturbing its complacency."[14]

Whether we call Bolingbroke an orator or a satirist, he matches Dixon's description. He uses the arts of rhetoric to persuade an audience to change its mind and accept his own ideas and beliefs. The particular rhetorical arts of self-presentation, irony, and the example will recur frequently in the following discussion of Bolingbroke's writing.

Chapter Three

Early Writings

Bolingbroke's earliest writings are four poems he wrote in his twenties and some unidentified contributions to *Poems on Affairs of State*, written at about the same time.[1] A brief political verse, first published in the *Craftsman* in 1730, and a conventional lover's address, "To Miss Lucy Atkins," written around 1700 but first published in 1758, complete Bolingbroke's poetic output. His talent for poetry was not great. His first published verse, "To Mr. Dryden," prefixed to Dryden's translation of Virgil (1697), is a mere conventional compliment to the great poet for whose commands the Muses wait, and who is crowned "wit's universal monarch." It is perhaps a sign of the young St. John's desire to rub shoulders with the great: at any rate, all these early poetic efforts were probably written because a fashionable young gentleman would be expected to "turn" a few verses.

A Letter to the Examiner and Other Pieces

We see no further sign of Bolingbroke's pen until 1710, the year in which the *Examiner* was begun. In the view of "the principal persons in power," the purpose of the new paper was publishing "just reflections upon former proceedings, and defending the present measures of her Majesty."[2] Bolingbroke was apparently one of five authors who wrote the first twelve papers before Swift took over the editorship and all of the writing. William King of Christ Church, Oxford, was the first editor and may have written nos. 5, 11, and 12. Samuel Garth and Matthew Prior wrote no. 6; Swift says that Bolingbroke, Francis Atterbury, and John Freind wrote the others, but we do not know precisely who wrote what.[3] All the early *Examiners* attempted to discredit the deposed Whigs in one way or another, by "exposing" their faulty logic, their misleading and loaded jargon, their alleged lies and sheer malice; or by arguing that money was now the source of power as a direct result of revolutionary principles and (what Swift and Bolingbroke disliked) that a lot of money was in the hands of the Whigs. The paper was a week old, in August 1710, when Bolingbroke wrote *A Letter to the Examiner*, which is something like a manifesto, urging Mr. Examiner to comment on the Whigs' policy of continuing the war of the Spanish Succession, and to expose their disloyalty to Queen Anne and their preference for encouraging faction.[4]

To expose the "*Factious Cabal*" (221) Bolingbroke employed simple propagandist techniques. The letter consists of a logical argument, taking as its starting point the letter by "Mr. Petticum" (actually a Whig apologist, possibly Arthur Maynwaring), whose politics the first and third issues of the *Examiner* had examined.[5] In that letter, Bolingbroke says, "How little Regard is paid to that Justness and Propriety of Character, without which, Compositions of this Kind are as Monstrous, as that Government must be, where Submission is made the Duty of the Prince, and Dominion the Prerogative of the Subject!" (221). Although his tone is not lofty, it does not descend to the conversational. Revealing that some people are trying to instigate a kind of revolution, Bolingbroke then denounces the former Whig ministers for "that Odium which [they] and their Faction, endeavour to throw on the QUEEN, and on those who have appear'd at her Call, and in her Defence" (222), but this odium will be turned on *them.*

Having established that his opponents are disloyal—and therefore, of course, untrustworthy and contemptible—Bolingbroke moves to a consideration of the war. Here he does adopt a relatively intimate tone, addressing Mr. Examiner directly. He uses a conventional satiric form established in several well-known political poems which instruct or advise a painter to depict the reality behind a military victory:[6]

> PAINT, Sir, with that Force which you are Master of, the present State of the War abroad, and expose to Publick View, those Principles, upon which it was Originally enter'd into. Collect some few of the Indignities which have been this Year offer'd to Her MAJESTY, and of those Unnatural Struggles, which have betray'd the Weakness of a shatter'd Constitution: And when this is done, *Dolben* shall blush in his Grave among the Dead, *Walpole* among the living, and even *Volpone* shall feel some Remorse. (222)[7]

So, the conduct of the war abroad has affected domestic affairs. The rest of the essay is a narrative showing that Britain has been exploited and duped even by her supposed allies, and for this Bolingbroke blames the Whigs of the previous administration. If this goes on, he says,

The *Dutch* will have a larger and a better Country than their Own, at the Expence of *Britain*, conquer'd for them, by those *Ministers*, who Once thought it Impolitick to Consent, that even *Ostend* should be made a Part of their Barrier.... *Britain* may expect to remain exhausted of Men and Money, to see her Trade divided amongst her Neighbours, her Revenues anticipated even to future Generations, and to have this only Glory left Her, that She has proved a Farm to the *Bank*, a Province of *Holland*, and a Jest to the whole world. (223–24)

The appeal is to the Briton's traditional chauvinism, but xenophobic or not, no one likes to look foolish. Having tried to stir his reader's anger and resentment, Bolingbroke modifies his tone in order to flatter the reader by appealing to his loyalty and wisdom: despite Whiggish arguments, "Mankind remains convinc'd, that a QUEEN possess'd of all the Vertues requisite to bless a Nation, or to make a private Family Happy, sits on the Throne" (224–25). By linking the queen with Tory policy, Bolingbroke links Whiggish opposition with disloyalty.

The rhetorical technique and the argument of the *Letter* are straightforward enough. Like all propagandists, Bolingbroke strives here to "prove" that he is right, but his attempt to do so is not to be found in the argument so much as in the essay's emotive appeals. At the end he tells Mr. Examiner:

if you would go to the Root of our Distemper, these are the Topicks you must insist upon, as the real Causes which have prolong'd the War, distracted the Nation, and given *France* Spirit enough at last to break off the *Peace*.

AND these are the Things, Sir, that deserve to pass under your Pen, that the Nation may be truly inform'd from what Springs our own Grievances, and the Hopes of our Enemies, have risen. (227)

The editor, then, will reveal the *real* causes, and the nation will therefore be *truly* informed. Even if Bolingbroke implies that every thinking man has already been persuaded that the case is obvious, he still wants such arguments to continue to appear in print, in keeping with the founders' purpose in starting the *Examiner.*

The *Examiner* itself claimed to have been launched at a time when the Court Whigs were still in power, and that it had consequently been instrumental in their downfall.[8] The last issue of the Whig paper, the *Medley*, exposed this fiction, by pointing out that the ministry had begun to crumble two months before the *Examiner* began. This apparently insignificant quibbling reveals that whoever launched the *Examiner* saw the press as a useful tool, not for bringing the Whigs down, but for keeping them down once they had fallen. It was Harley, not Bolingbroke, who launched the *Examiner.* It was also largely Harley's doing that a newspaper stamp tax was introduced in 1712. The tax has usually been seen as an attempt to exercise some control over opposition papers. Although Bolingbroke had conceived much earlier of a tax for this purpose, Harley's conception was of a measure to bring in some revenue. His intention seems not to have been to silence his opposition, but to have at his disposal a press that would justify his ministry. Bolingbroke's attitude, on the other hand, was far more extreme. The *Letter to the Examiner* embodies an extremism that Harley is unlikely to have approved or endorsed, and it seems probable that Bolingbroke had in mind a much wider censorship, extending perhaps to the total silencing of all opposition.

During his four years in office as Secretary of State under Queen Anne, Bolingbroke hoped to keep the ministry's opponents in the press quiet, and in the absence of rigid controls, one method of doing so was to arrest and prosecute printers and journalists. The poorly defined libel laws, however, enabled many of his victims to escape. In the late 1720s Bolingbroke led a campaign against Walpole that exploited the press and profited deliberately from the same weakness in the law.

While Bolingbroke looked for various ways to keep the opposition Whigs under restraint, the ministry had to be positively justified. Among the many pamphlets that did so, one has always commanded attention: *The Conduct of the Allies* (1711). The language of Swift's enormously popular pamphlet is sometimes strikingly close to that of *A Letter to the Examiner*, but in a more general way Swift sought to justify the secretary by arguing that his attempts to secure peace were being hampered by the actions of a factious cabal—and that, therefore, was why so little had come of the negotiations.

Bolingbroke's several attempts at self-justification may suggest the anxieties of an insecure man. Politically, that is precisely what he became as Queen Anne neared her death in 1714. Although it may be true that his "role in relation to the press," as J. A. Downie puts it, "was a minor one,"[9] it is clear that Bolingbroke relied considerably on journalism and propaganda to consolidate what power he had.

Self-justification emerges again as the theme of two short pieces by Bolingbroke printed in 1715. One was *The Representation.* In this formal, prepared speech Bolingbroke presented to the House of Lords, in February 1714, "the present state of the several Treaties of Her Majesty, and Her Allies with *France* and *Spain.*"[10] He felt he needed to defend the length of time taken to bring about peace. Negotiations had begun in April 1711, yet the Treaty of Utrecht was not concluded until July 1713. It had taken so long, he said with more than a hint of xenophobia, because even Britain's allies had been double-dealing, obstructing negotiations out of pure self-interest. Bolingbroke relates how "the whole Confederacy was industriously alarm'd, Jealousies were every where sown, and even in *Britain* the most licentious Clamours were raised against Her Majesty's Proceedings" (7). He accuses the Dutch of hypocrisy and the Germans of plain obstinacy. The war was impracticable because it was so expensive, yet although Germany had no intention of paying, and Austria's financial contribution was negligible, the Emperor was determined to prolong the war. The Netherlands, said Bolingbroke with a devastating rhetorical display,

> bore a considerable Burthen; but as they had, from the Year 1708, sent no Supplies, of any kind, either to *Portugal*, or to *Catalonia*, and had drawn themselves almost entirely out of the *Spanish* War; as they furnish'd, in no Proportion, their Quota for the Sea-Service; as they had reduc'd their Joint-Contributions with the Queen, in all Payments, to One-Third of the Whole; and, as they were very backward in answering even this Share of Expence, so the Load of *Great Britain* came, upon their Account, as well as upon the Emperor's, to be vastly encreas'd. As to the rest of the Allies, all the Troops which they furnish'd, were maintain'd by the Queen, and the States, except a few, and those almost employ'd in Covering their own Frontiers. (9–10)

Among the statements of what the Dutch did and did not do, the generous opening sentence, that they "bore a considerable Burthen," is soon lost in Bolingbroke's controlled sarcasm. The main point of this passage, as of most of the speech, is that Britain is left by her allies to pay all the bills, while the allies pursue selfish ends. This argument had been heard before in *The Conduct of the Allies*, and the general election of 1710 had been fought at least partly over such an issue.[11]

This speech has one other purpose. When the Catalans had rebelled against Spain, the allied powers—Britain among them—had supported the rebellion as a means to oppose France, but the Treaty of Utrecht denied the Catalans any degree of independence. In the last part of his speech Bolingbroke defends the British government's attitude against accusations of broken promises and betrayal. One anonymous author, delighted by Bolingbroke's flight to France in 1715, was obviously not impressed by Bolingbroke's defense of the ministry's treatment of the Catalans: "Rouze, O ye Ghosts of the murder'd *Catalans*, who were barbarously Betray'd, while ye valiantly Fought in the Defence of your Ancient Liberties: Heaven at last will avenge your Blood."[12]

Generally, Bolingbroke's speech is relatively low-toned, void of eloquent oratory. Instead Bolingbroke tries to sound reasonable and cool, making a careful survey of events and finally blaming everyone but the British for the delay and expense of obtaining peace. Since he was one of the principal negotiators, the speech can be seen as a piece of self-justification; still, the dominant features of the text are its clarity and logic. Bolingbroke argues his case in favor of Britain by saying, in effect, "it is not our fault, yet still we have reached a good solution," and by emphasizing again that even allies (perhaps all foreigners) are seldom dependable. And he ensures as usual that he himself emerges from the atmosphere of disunion and distrust with some distinction.

The other work of 1715 is *A Copy of My Lord Bolingbroke's Letter to My Lord—*(in fact addressed to Lord Lansdowne).[13] This very brief letter is a statement of explicit and challenging self-defense, on the subject of Bolingbroke's hasty departure from England. "Had there been the least Reason to hope for a fair and open Trial," he says, "after having been already prejudg'd, unheard by the two Houses of Parliament, I should not have declined the strictest Examination" and he challenges his enemies to prove his corruption or criminal correspondence. The letter finishes with a straightforward testimony of loyalty to the late Queen and to his country.[14] One contemporary noted that "this Letter is plainly calculated to draw an *Odium* on the present Administration, and the faithful Representatives of the whole Kingdom."[15] Generally, however, the *Letter* has attracted very little attention.

A Letter to Sir William Windham

Between his flight in 1715 and his return to active political life in England in 1726, Bolingbroke wrote only one political work, *A Letter to Sir William Windham* (1717). This prose tract, which he called "a monument of my justification to posterity,"[16] was an attempt to improve his battered reputation.

This work failed to evoke much enthusiasm among the leading Tories whom it was meant to impress. Not much notice was taken of it when it was eventually published in 1753, but it has pleased later critics. Geoffrey Butler thought Bolingbroke's language of "witty scorn" had been "rarely if ever surpassed in political writing."[17] And Paul Baratier and H. T. Dickinson both consider the *Letter* a powerful work.[18]

The *Letter* falls into three parts. About one third of the essay describes the circumstances of the ministry from 1710 to 1714, leading to Bolingbroke's decision to flee the country; a shorter section follows, describing the Pretender's attempted invasion, and a lengthy final section is devoted to a portrait of the Pretender, a description of a smear campaign directed at Bolingbroke, and Bolingbroke's advice to the Tory party.

Beneath the first section is an impulse to lay the blame for Britain's troubles on the unhealthy divisiveness of parties. This impulse, possibly an ad hoc solution to the problem of plausibly justifying his conduct, was to become central to Bolingbroke's political thinking. When Bolingbroke returned to the subject of the last years of Anne's reign in *The State of Parties at the Accession of King George I* (written about 1739, published 1749), he repeated his argument that party divisions cause national disorders. In the later essay he called for the destruction of faction and its replacement by true union and patriotism: his concentration on these subjects gives the work a less personal concern than the *Letter to Windham.*

Bolingbroke's method of self-defense in the *Letter* is to spread the blame: "I am afraid that we came to court [in 1710] in the same dispositions as all parties have done . . . that our principal views were the conservation of this power [of government], great employments to ourselves, and great opportunities of rewarding those who had helped to raise us, and of hurting those who stood in opposition to us" (114). As the essay progresses, with Bolingbroke supposedly apologizing to the Tories for his own part in what happened under the ministry, he keeps himself curiously in the background, and it is not long before he is accusing the Whigs of prolonging the war for financial gain. Merchants and landowners, he says, lost a great amount of money through the war, "whilst the lender of money, who added nothing to the common stock, throve by the public calamity, and contributed not a mite to the public charge" (116). Soon, the earl of Oxford becomes a public figure of incompetence (117), responsible for the neglect of government. As the ministry and the party "grew weaker every day" the peace, "the very work, which ought to have been the basis of our strength, was in part demolished before our eyes, and we were stoned with the ruins of it. Whilst this was doing, Oxford looked on, . . . and on those occasions, where his station obliged him to speak of business, was absolutely unintelligible. . . . I am sorry to be obliged to name him so often; but how is it possible to do otherwise, while I am speaking of times wherein the whole turn of affairs depended on his motions and character?" (121–22).

The tone of these early passages reveals Bolingbroke as a minister laboring under enormously difficult burdens because Oxford had shirked his responsibilities: "To those who had the opportunity of looking behind the curtain I may likewise appeal for the difficulties which lay in my way, and for the particular discouragements which I met with" (117). He goes on to declare his "unfashionable" sentiments, explaining how he swallowed his resentment and allowed loyalty to prevail (118) when the queen "treated me ill," and he indicates his own high-mindedness in not taking an idealistic view of the treaties or of their negotiation. The impression he creates over these early pages is that everyone is to blame but himself: he presents himself as an almost tragic hero caught in a web of events and forces over which he has little control. From the Whigs' endeavor "to expose me for a fool, and to brand me for a knave" (112–13), and his *ex post facto* reflection on this, "But then I had deserved this abundantly at their hands, according to the notions of party-justice," he travels a long way in a few pages, to a position from which he criticizes the frenzied prattle of the Tory party that had no policy to articulate in debates on the succession (121). Preferring not to remind his readers that he was—or should have been—a policy maker, he draws attention instead to the party's disunity and the selfishness and incompetence of Oxford.

So far, Bolingbroke appears to be a narrator whose sincerity may not be trusted. Again and again he courts his reader's sympathy. In his description of the Pretender's misguided preparations for his invasion, Bolingbroke presents himself as the able counselor that he was, offering sensible advice that the foolish James rejected. Where Bolingbroke casts himself in the role of the injured innocent, finally excluded from James's affairs and used as a scapegoat, his picture of his relations with the Pretender is near the truth. Speaking of his relations with two other prominent Jacobites, Bolingbroke repeats his tactic, but with rather less historical accuracy: "those persons whom the Duke of Ormond and the Earl of Mar must influence, or might silence, were the loudest in defaming me. . . . This method of beating down the reputation of a man by noise and impudence, imposed on the world at first, convinced people who were not acquainted with me, and staggered even my friends. But it ceased in a few days to have any effect against me. The malice was too gross to pass upon reflection" (159). Bolingbroke here shifts the focus of justification, seeming to establish his own integrity by blackening his malicious enemies. It is a rhetorical method that he repeats in a somewhat wider appeal to leading Tories: "The whigs may continue inveterate, and by consequence frustrate his majesty's good intentions towards me; the tories may continue to rail at me, on the credit of such enemies as I have described to you in the course of this relation: neither the one nor the other shall make me swerve out of the path which I have traced to myself" (166). This is a reminder to the Tories to be loyal to George I and therefore to have no truck with Jacobitism. A part of the same concept is his warning that the Tories should not listen to the unimaginative products of the Jacobite propaganda machine, whose aim is only "that of poisoning the minds of the tories . . . against me" (167). All of this implicitly places Bolingbroke on the side of innocence, virtue, and the king's *good* intentions. Anyone who still censures Bolingbroke is therefore misguided, unfair, and wrong.

Throughout his treatment of the character of the Pretender and his supporters, Bolingbroke seeks to show that it is in their interests to pour infamy on him. This section of the narrative dissociates Bolingbroke from Jacobitism, admitting his "crimes" (167) but trying to show that he has been the unfortunate victim of folly and malice.

For the planned landing of rebel forces in Scotland, the kings of Sweden and France—despite their promises of help—provided no money, no troops, no arms, and no ammunition (155). Yet, says Bolingbroke, the Jacobites said "the war in Scotland . . . might have been supported, and might have succeeded too, if I had procured the succors which were asked, nay, if I had sent a little powder" (160). It was actually beyond his power to obtain these "succors," but the Jacobite propaganda held that "these succors might have been obtained, and a proof that they might, is, that they were so by others. These people leave the cause of this mismanagement doubtful, between my treachery and my want of capacity. The Pretender, with all the false charity and real malice of one who sets up for devotion, attributes all his misfortunes to my negligence" (160). From a position of self-justification, which one would normally expect to be defensive, Bolingbroke has turned to outright aggression, damning Oxford, the Pretender, and those Tories who resent him because those so-called Tories are now Jacobites. To have any chance of rebuilding his career, Bolingbroke has to show that he has renounced Jacobitism, and his strategy in this *Letter* is to show how badly he was treated by the Pretender (hence a personal motive for abandoning the Jacobite cause) and how useful he is in revealing the truth about the Pretender and the cause (hence a political motive). The Pretender emerges as a bigot, a fool, and a fanatic, Bolingbroke as a cool, honest, determined man whose experience and patriotism will now be more serviceable. He thinks this contrast will prove his "crimes" not "to be of a very black dye" (167). His purpose is therefore twofold. He seeks to unite the disunited Tory party, without its Jacobite wing, by suggesting that Britain under the Pretender would rapidly degenerate into slavery or anarchy (178). He also seeks to show that his own errors and excesses were the results not of personal malice or lack of principle, but of difficulties thrown upon him by his enemies. The climax of the *Letter* is no longer a traitor's apology, but a recognition of political realities.

Since Bolingbroke intends to justify himself to politicians who might help to reinstate him, *A Letter to Sir William Windham* inevitably contains a strong personal element and is inevitably concerned with improving Bolingbroke's tarnished image. He throws himself at the feet of those who can save him, justifies himself with a show of repentance for past crimes (which he claims were not really his responsibility), and commends himself as a useful ally by contrasting himself with a man of considerable intellectual limitations. That his method was overtly rhetorical was noticed by one contemporary commentator, who remarked acidly that "it has been seldom found, that a fine writer or great orator was a man of the most solid judgment in politicks," and in the *Letter* Bolingbroke "has shewn so much satryrical wit, and severity of expression, both against the Jacobites, and the person of the *Pretender*, that it very much derogates from his credit as to the facts he relates. Such sort of rhetorick might do very well in a speech to a popular assembly, made on purpose to inflame, and to provoke them to some hasty resolution."[19] Bolingbroke mistakenly thought he could shake off the stigma of his period of blatant Jacobitism, but he continued to be regarded with suspicion despite the rhetorical creation of his new, more attractive self.

This technique of apparent sincerity, and the suspicion that it so often arouses, added to Bolingbroke's unwanted reputation for opportunism and hypocrisy. When he was "exiled" from Parliament after losing his seat in 1708, he indulged in another, private kind of hypocrisy, writing from Bucklebury to his friends that he enjoyed the retired life and was glad to be out of politics. Now, during his exile in France, he did the same. It was hardly plausible that he should enjoy being away from the life he was impatiently trying to regain.[20]

On 1 January 1722 Bolingbroke told Swift, "I have lately wrot an excellent treatise," *Reflections upon Exile*,[21] which argues that exile is so far from intolerable that it actually has many attractions. The treatise was apparently not intended for publication, but written only to help Lady Bolingbroke improve her English.[22] *Reflections* was generally well received.[23]

The whole essay, a loose imitation and paraphrase of Seneca's *Consolatio ad Helviam*, puts forward a few simple points. Any man who never expects good fortune will never suffer the disappointment of ill fortune. Bolingbroke goes on to ask: what, really, is exile? His answer is: change of place, plus a few material losses. But it is not really so intolerable to live deprived of one's country: millions do so voluntarily. What, he asks, is so special about one piece of land? The whole short essay is an exercise in stoic philosophy, arguing that reason will conquer disappointments, unless a man is tame enough to submit to time. The *Reflections* suggest that the author may be putting on a brave face to conceal his frustrations.

Beginnings of Philosophy

Bolingbroke's association with the Abbé Alary, and later with the Club de l'Entresol, stimulated in Bolingbroke a desire to be a philosopher. On 1 July, N.S., 1719 he told Alary, "There is nothing so worthy of man as a sincere search for truth."[24] Certainly he kept Alary informed of his projects and his ideas, and on 26 April, N.S., 1722 he told the Abbé that he was bringing to a close two years' work by defining the limits of knowledge, and that he would soon start on a project he had had "running through my head for a long time," a history of both Rome and Britain.[25] How easy it is, he says, to acquire the truth! He tells Alary also that it was the members of the Club de l'Entresol who "confirmed my taste for philosophy,"[26] and for them Bolingbroke wrote *Reflections concerning Innate Moral Principles.*[27] An early—and simple—attempt at philosophical writing, this treatise tries to prove that compassion, though considered to be innate, is something we acquire through custom and education. Self-love, says Bolingbroke, is innate and would threaten to lead men out of control, were it not for the savior, reason.

Bolingbroke's "proof" that love for one's parents and compassion for one's fellowmen is not innate is of a kind that provoked a furor over his later writings:

> Do we mean then that this Proposition, "It is the Duty of a Child to respect and love his Father," and this other, "It is the Duty of a Man to pity and help his Fellow," are two Truths imprinted by God on the Understanding of every Man, at the Moment of giving him Being? That would be too absurd; because the Ideas of Relation, as well as the other Ideas which join to compound these Propositions, are not innate, and consequently the Truths which they contain cannot be innate.... For if those Principles of Action are placed in all Men, why do they not discover themselves in all Men by their Effects? (13–17)

And so, nothing is demonstrably innate until we observe "that it is common to all Men, and constant in it's [*sic*] Operation" (17). Bolingbroke's argumentative method seems often to be deduction not from indisputable fact or axiom, but from personal belief. Although not a very important piece, the pamphlet indicates the development of a more philosophical turn of mind. Here, inspired by some of the leading thinkers in France, Bolingbroke is searching for truth:

> Compassion happens to be thought innate, like many other things that have as weak a Title, only because we do not remember it's [*sic*] Birth, and because it is much easier to say that a thing is innate, and to sit down quietly in a vulgar Error, which few will take the trouble to overturn, than to search out with Care and Accuracy the Beginning and the Progress of such a thing, and to pursue Truth through such untrodden Ways as few know, and many shun through Prejudice. (11)

But apart from this healthy skepticism, the essay also contains observations that, when repeated in his later work, damaged his reputation severely. Bolingbroke observes, for example, that "Even among the Christians themselves, the enlightened, sanctified, elect Christians, those happy Mortals, who alone know that Name by which alone Men can be saved, how many Instances of Cruelty, how few of Compassion do we find!" (27) and he points out that Christians have never hesitated to indulge in wholesale carnage (27). Such outspoken remarks as these are part of his strategy of listing instances where compassion is not to be seen, in order to argue that, if it cannot be seen, it cannot be innate.

Conclusions

This collection of early prose pieces, slight by comparison with what was to follow, marked the end of a phase of his career in which Bolingbroke reached the highest and lowest points on the wheel of fortune. The writings themselves reveal occasional glimpses of his literary talent and of his ability to transpose the rhetoric of oratory into the contemporary market for pamphlets and newspapers. His exile in France enabled him to add to this nucleus the benefit of conversation about and learning in philosophy, history, and literature.

Putting the combined experience of those years to good use, he returned to conduct a campaign of opposition to Walpole's ministry. Despite continual frustration, Bolingbroke and his circle opposed Walpole with sophisticated and coherent political theory, historiographical argument, and a range of literary devices.

There are signs in the *Letter to Sir William Windham* that the desire for self-justification gives way to a more aggressive impulse. The *Letter*'s failure to stir much Tory enthusiasm may have convinced Bolingbroke that continual defensive self-justification was not the effective weapon he had once thought it, for he played it down during the next phase of his career, when he moved into the more obviously aggressive position of a virtual leader of opposition.

Both in and out of power, Bolingbroke repeatedly attempted to put himself in a position where, to a social or political circle, he was indispensable, or at least influential, giving incentives to those around him. Instead of justifying his conduct, the members of his circles were supposed to regard him as the sage whose ideas they would propagate. This idea is expressed in his self-commendation to the Tories, in the letter to Wyndham. Bolingbroke seems to have realized that the best way to distract attention from the stigma of his apparently unacceptable Jacobitism was neither to apologize nor to defend his behavior, but to launch a scathing broadside attack on his enemies. This, with the help of the ablest writers of the day, is what Bolingbroke proceeded to do.

Chapter Four

The Politics of Liberty

On 5 December 1726 a few copies could be had of a new periodical, the *Craftsman*, by Caleb D'Anvers of Gray's Inn, Esquire. For five months this sheet was published twice a week. Its four columns contained, like the well-known *Tatler* or *Spectator* papers, an essay, or sometimes a small miscellany of essays or letters. From no. 45 (13 May 1727) the paper became more than twice as large, printed on a crown sheet folded once, still containing essays and also news and two pages of advertisements; the title was altered significantly to *The Country Journal: or, the Craftsman.* The paper was now a newspaper with a leading article, and it purported to represent the "country" interest—that is, the gentry, the "squirearchy," or, more generally, the opposition to the "court" party led by Walpole. In precisely this form, the *Craftsman* continued for another twenty-five years.[1]

The *Craftsman* was begun by Bolingbroke and Pulteney, and they appointed as editor Nicholas Amhurst, a Whig hack writer who had been expelled from Oxford in 1721. In the paper's first decade, while Bolingbroke was its leading contributor, the *Craftsman* became the best-selling newspaper of the age, with a top circulation of around 13,000 in 1731 and little less than 10,000 at any time between 1729 and 1732.[2] It was read all over Europe, printed in French, and published in Amsterdam; it was passed around in the coffeehouses and industriously distributed throughout England; its articles were reprinted in the provincial press and in New York and even read aloud to the illiterate. The aim stated in the first issue was to expose political craft, but the real purpose was simply to remove Walpole from office and repair the declining state of the nation. To achieve these aims, the writers had to appeal to as broad a readership as possible: to members of Parliament, merchants and traders, landowners, and even the *beau monde.* With a diversity of people to be addressed, influenced, and if possible converted, the several authors were obliged to write in several different styles and forms on a fairly wide range of subjects.

To understand Bolingbroke's part in the *Craftsman*, some attention must be paid to the paper as a whole, and not just to Bolingbroke's own contributions in isolation.

Caleb D'Anvers of Gray's Inn, Esquire

In "Caleb" and "Craftsman," the founders chose two appropriate biblical echoes to emphasize Caleb D'Anvers' role as the leader of renovation and to indicate his own craftsmanship, together with the corruptions—principally financial—of his fellow craftsmen. In the book of Numbers, Caleb, son of Jephunneh, is sent into Canaan to spy out the land (13: 2, 6), which he exhorts the Israelites to "go up at once, and possess" (13: 30). He despairs, with Moses, Aaron, and Joshua, when the people reject this exhortation (14: 1–10). For his persistence, Caleb is favored by God (14: 24). In addition, Caleb's qualities are reflected by the Hebrew form of the name, which indicates fidelity, tenacity, and even honor.[3] The total implication is obvious: Caleb is a loyal leader, faithful to a cause.

As for "Craftsman," it is likely that a parallel was intended with this passage from the New Testament:

> For a certain man named Demetrius, a silversmith, which made silver shrines for Diana, brought no small gain unto the craftsmen;
> Whom he called together with the workmen of like occupation, and said, Sirs, ye know that by this craft we have our wealth.
> Moreover ye see and hear, that not alone at Ephesus, but almost throughout all Asia, this Paul hath persuaded and turned away much people, saying that they be no gods, which are made with hands:
> So that not only this our craft is in danger to be set at nought; but also that the temple of the great goddess Diana should be despised, and her magnificence should be destroyed, whom all Asia and the world worshippeth.[4]

Corrupt craftsmen worship false idols, from which they amass wealth, and they oppose the leader, whose integrity threatens their very existence.

Why D'Anvers? In *Craftsman* 29 (20 March 1727) the pseudonymous author declares that his name is derived from the French "de Anvers," that is, from Antwerp. The argument is that because Antwerp is held by the Holy Roman Emperor, Caleb is a supporter of the German interest and therefore of the Hanoverian Succession. At least "Caleb D'Anvers of Gray's Inn, Esquire," had the right tone of the experienced gentleman. The first essay introduced this wise old fellow. Caleb D'Anvers was a less prominent figure than his predecessors in the polite periodicals—Isaac Bickerstaff in the *Tatler*, for example—but he was important. He was obviously a screen to conceal the identities of the paper's contributors, but he could also usefully break down the barrier between the author and the reader. Rapport between author and reader involves courting the reader's sympathy, which is crucial if a political periodical is to get its ideas widely accepted. One technique to break down the barrier and establish rapport between the author and the reader is that of epistolary fiction, in which the relationship of the real author to the reader becomes concurrent with that of the fictional author to the reader.[5] For four years Caleb D'Anvers's role was stressed: he says a few things about himself, interposes with a comment from time to time, qualifies a distinction, or pauses to define a term, but in particular many papers take the form of letters to him. Most of Bolingbroke's contributions to the *Craftsman*, like nearly all his other works, take the form of letters.

In no. 25 (3 March 1727), Bolingbroke's second contribution, Caleb D'Anvers, declaring his intention "to pay the utmost Regard to all the kind assistances of my Correspondents," introduces a letter that tells Mr. D'Anvers about the mismanagement of his "several *Plantations* in the *West-India* Colonies," (V, 3) in the corrupt control of his steward, who oppresses D'Anvers's tenants for the sake of enriching himself. If "*sinister Designs*" such as this are opposed by the tenants, the stewards who execute the designs habitually "load your *Tenants* with terms of reproach, such as *seditious, turbulent Spirits, Jacobites*, and other such opprobrious names, as they imagine will render them obnoxious to your *self* or your *Domesticks*" (V, 6). Two points emerge from this. First, a correspondent is needed to provide Caleb D'Anvers with information about his own estates: the letter is strictly narrative and informative, and therefore is analogous to the kind of letter that a genuine estate owner might expect to receive from a sympathetic informer. Its being a letter to him places Caleb and the reader of the paper in identical positions. This *Craftsman* therefore encourages the reader to feel a sense of outrage (as Caleb would) and to take decisive action to prevent corruption. If the reader could be actively encouraged, the paper was becoming effective in arousing opposition to Walpole, for the second point is that Walpole and the steward are synonymous. By aligning Walpole with a crooked steward, the letter plays with an established hatred of stewards and gives it a precisely political turn. Walpole's reaction to any opposition, Bolingbroke says, is to brand all his opponents with the defamatory label of "Jacobites."

Three weeks later Bolingbroke wrote another letter to Caleb D'Anvers. It was another account of corruption and the pursuit of private interest among Mr. D'Anvers's servants:

> I could wish, *Sir*, that you would now and then, of an Evening, come *incog.* to the publick Coffee Houses, as some of your Predecessors have done; for then you will be truly informed, of the Opinions and Sentiments of Mankind, who cannot be suspected of any sinister designs, since you will, by *those* Means, be unknown to them.
>
> It was pleasant enough, the other day, to hear of one of your *Menial Servants*, a Creature of ROBIN'S, after many invectives, and base insinuations, assert, with a confident air, that you are not the Author of the *Craftsman*, but that those Papers are written by some of your *discarded Servants*, to vent their *Spleen* and *Malice*, and that they impose upon the World, by prefixing your Name to them; Nay, He had the assurance to mention some particular persons, who are not only incapable of any Low designs, but are as eminent for Their *wit* and *fine* parts, as for their *probity* and *untainted virtue*. (no. 30, 20 March 1727; V, 8)

The implication is that the menial servant is laughably wrong to suppose that anyone other than Caleb D'Anvers writes the paper. At the same time this implication is palpably disingenuous, since it was an open secret that Bolingbroke and Pulteney were involved with the *Craftsman*. "Robin" had been introduced in the first issue, and subsequent papers repeated his function as Caleb's servant. "Robin" was one of Walpole's many nicknames, so that there is a perceptible parallel here which hints that Caleb represents the people who elect and employ Walpole. Caleb's discarded servants would then indicate both Pulteney and Bolingbroke. In the preceding paragraph Caleb is invited to participate in real London life to hear popular opinion, and by doing so he will imitate some of his "Predecessors," such as Mr. Spectator. Caleb is therefore placed simultaneously in a polite, fictitious tradition and in a real coffeehouse, where real opinions are expressed, including those about the authors of the *Craftsman*. The insistence that Caleb D'Anvers is the sole author of the paper, as well as the use of a letter to him, helps to create sympathy between Caleb and the reader. Since, moreover, Caleb is the employer whose trust and money are abused by Walpole for selfish ends, the reader also becomes aware, by this close identification with Caleb, that he is himself being cheated. The gradual development of Caleb D'Anvers's character perpetuates this sympathy, with the obvious intention of establishing the reader's political sympathy.

In the *Remarks on the History of England*, a series of letters, D'Anvers learns about the history of England in the same way as he learns about trouble on his plantations. The letters use the same technique of attracting the reader to Caleb's position. Bolingbroke, the author of all these pieces, comments (in no. 206, 13 June 1730) about the *Craftsman*'s ability to arouse active interest and inquiry as well as to impart a sense of urgency to its readers. Such a sense arises as much from Caleb D'Anvers's character as from his writings. Having defined him as the leader of the opposition to Walpole, the paper gives its sympathetic readers the chance to consider themselves as a part of that opposing movement. It persuades them to express themselves, as many readers did by sending contributions to the printer.

The authors of the *Craftsman* realized that, to be effective, their journalism had to attract the votes of independent freeholders and Whigs in Parliament. With the parliamentary opposition disunited, opposition in the nation as a whole tended to be disunited. Whigs never rallied around Bolingbroke, nor Tories around Pulteney, while Jacobites supported only themselves and the Pretender. The *Craftsman* never carried only Bolingbroke's flag, nor only Pulteney's, and it gained from its tactful dissociation from the Jacobites: instead, to appeal to a wide readership, it proposed a type of moderation. One solution to the problem of uniting diverse and independent elements was Caleb D'Anvers. His biblical name and its echo; his diversity of approaches and methods; his political wisdom; his receipt of hundreds of letters, all made him a total symbol of the *cause* of opposition to Walpole. Caleb D'Anvers emphasized his moderation by refusing to embrace arguments that did not rely on the force of reason. It was fitting that he should become such a symbol, combining both Bolingbroke's ambitions and Pulteney's parliamentary activity. To Bolingbroke, in particular, the fictional editor provided a sobriety, a stability of temperament that the "mercurial" lord did not possess.

Bolingbroke was known to write for the *Craftsman*, but his previous public conduct would hamper a concerted campaign of opposition. He (and the other authors) therefore became Caleb D'Anvers or one of his correspondents, yet even this strategy could not bring Bolingbroke what he most needed, trust.

Bolingbroke's Miscellaneous Contributions to the *Craftsman*, 1726–1731

Early numbers of the *Craftsman* ensured that whatever forms or subjects appeared, readers would be trained in the art of recognizing irony. Thus the accepted way of accusing Walpole of lying, cheating, and robbing soon became: "the *Ministry* . . . are all *just Stewards, gracious Magistrates, uncorrupt Administrators* of publick Money . . . quite the contrary to what I have endeavour'd to expose." In case the point was still not clear enough, Caleb D'Anvers drew attention to his rhetorical use and conception of irony:

> I am confident that every Man will acquit me of such a Design, who knows what *Irony* means, and that it is a *Figure* in *Rhetorick*, by which we may ridicule any Person, by praising him for Qualities, of which He is known to be destitute, or for the contraries of which He is remarkable. . . . It could not therefore be my Design, in any of the preceding Papers, to asperse the present Administration, in an ironical manner, without being guilty of so great a Weakness as to imagine, that I could impose characters upon the World, of which Those Gentlemen are a living and exemplary Confutation. (no. 18, 7 February 1727)

With this obvious ironical posture unambiguously set out, the paper gradually developed its own mythology, making use of traditions of allegory, fable, and fictional visions; the contemporary theater (as an analogue of government); the Theophrastan character; and a "golden age" in which Satan and Mammon came to be identified with Walpole. In addition, many contributions are simply argumentative essays against pro-government journals, and many more are concerned with trade and the British constitution. Most of Bolingbroke's miscellaneous contributions concern these last two subjects. However, his best known single *Craftsman* paper is a fictional vision.

Bolingbroke's first contribution to the *Craftsman* was printed in no. 16, on 27 January 1727, as "The First Vision of Camilick." Caleb D'Anvers, expecting "grave discourses on publick matters" during the new parliamentary session, decides to present "something, which has no relation at all to public affairs, but is of a nature purely amusing, and entirely void of reflection upon any person whatsoever." This irony—the first satirical pointer—introduces the vision, which has supposedly been translated from an oriental manuscript and presented to the public by courtesy of its owner, Mr. D'Anvers.

The vision concerns two rival armies, one bearing warlike insignia, the other carrying "emblematical figures of justice, peace, law, and liberty." The latter army is guided by "a large roll of parchment" that a king is seen to sign, whereupon it flies "up into the air ... encompassed with rays of glory." In the abrupt manner of a dream, the scene shifts: "Soon after, I saw both of these hosts engaged, and the whole face of the land overspread with blood. I saw the king who had signed and broken that sacred charter, drink out of a golden cup, fall into convulsions, gasp and die" (*Works*, 1:236–37). Then the armies fight again, despite another king's promise "to make the words contained in the roll the guide of his actions." This king is taken prisoner, but his son relieves him, executing "the chiefs of the other army." Other bloody battles ensue; but as long as the parchment is visible, "those heroes, who fought beneath it" never give up. "At last the long contention ceased," and peace, harmony, and union prevail:

> I saw one king twelve times bow down before the bright phenomenon, which from thenceforward spread a light over the whole land; and, descending nearer to the earth, the beams of it grew so warm as it approached, that the hearts of the inhabitants leaped for joy. The face of war was no more.... Plenty laughed in the valleys. Industry, commerce, and liberty danced hand in hand throughout the cities. (1:237)

Again the scene changes, and this "amiable prospect" is replaced by "a large and magnificent hall, resembling the great divan or council of the nation." Here "The nobles of the land were ... assembled" (237) to sing in praise of their parchment, after which "all the rulers took a solemn oath to preserve it inviolate and unchanged" (238). A second assembly joins the first, sings to much the same purpose, and curses anyone who should violate the words of the roll. However, they are interrupted by "a man, dressed in a plain habit, with a purse of gold in his hand," who surveys them with "A smile, or rather a sneer," but "they all turned their faces from the canopy, and fell prostrate before him. He trod over their backs," scattering gold everywhere, and "seized ... the sacred parchment itself.

He rumpled it rudely up, and crammed it into his pocket." This action raises murmurs, but they are silenced by more gold. The disappearance of the parchment causes "half the august assembly" to be at once "in chains" (238).

The allegory is simple. The parchment is Magna Carta, and the king who signs it must therefore be John. Charles I is the captive king, Charles II his rescuer. Both vow to follow the dictates of Magna Carta, yet actually ignore it. It is under William III that Britain flourishes in peace, when the Houses of Parliament express their reverent respect for the principles of liberty. Walpole, popularly nicknamed "brass face" or "brazen face" is recognizably the ruffian, his "face bronzed over with a glare of confidence" (238). When Magna Carta is crushed and pocketed, to be replaced by Walpole's gold, Britain's liberty disappears. Church and state are alike subjected to slavery as "Pontiffs . . . and senators" are "linked together like the most ignominious slaves" (238).

This caricature history of England does not describe only Walpole's rise to power. It also contains a simple warning that Walpole's power depends on his supply of money; for as soon as he drops his purse, "He himself dropt with it to the ground; that and the date of his power at once expired; He sunk, and sunk for ever" (238). Liberty is at once restored, the scroll resuming its place in the air, and the vision ends with biblical resonance: "the HEART OF THE KING WAS GLAD WITHIN HIM" (239).

The headnote of this essay is "In Hoc Signo vinces" ("by this sign you shall conquer"). These words were inscribed on the cross Constantine the Great saw in a vision before the battle of Milvian Bridge in 312, when he defeated the tyrant Maxentius and became converted to Christianity. Constantine's advisers interpreted the vision as a sign of triumph over death, and the trophy of the cross became the labarum, the emperor's symbol of Christian victory over his enemies. As Constantine's statue in Rome states that the labarum is the badge of Christian valor, so those who fight for the parchment, in Bolingbroke's essay, are "heroes." Constantine delivered Rome from tyranny: Walpole's departure restores liberty and defeats slavery. Further parallels indicate that Magna Carta is not only the symbol and foundation of liberty, but also a symbol of Christian strength and hope against tyranny. Walpole, of course, is the tyrant.

This popular essay is a manifesto of Bolingbroke's political opposition to Walpole. Aside from conveying Bolingbroke's customary disapproval of the weak Stuart kings and his tactful praise of William III, the essay clearly states Bolingbroke's view that some members of Parliament are shamefully enslaved by money and that Walpole is cynical and ruthless, but that his power is dependent solely on money. The essay also shows that Bolingbroke, like the other authors of the *Craftsman*, defends the cause of righteousness and liberty, defying all that Walpole can do. The "great man's" instant response was to issue a warrant for the arrest of all concerned in the printing of this paper, but nothing could be pinned on them.

The fictional method of this essay, which J. H. Plumb calls "a simple, slapstick personal satire of Walpole,"[6] is not typical of Bolingbroke's essays in the *Craftsman*. However, the central subjects of most of his miscellaneous essays are, as here, the constitution and wealth, and "The First Vision of Camilick" is typical in revealing Bolingbroke's belief that his country is in decline, morally, socially, and politically. He states this belief succinctly in the first of his three *Occasional Writer* essays (1727),[7] arguing that Walpole's foreign policy is founded on immorality, which is bad enough, but the immediate consequence is that commerce suffers. Bolingbroke blames Walpole for jeopardizing the "very principle for which we have fought ever since the revolution [of 1688]" and for undoing the advantages of the Utrecht settlement.[8] Bolingbroke was anxious to preserve the rights won in 1688: liberty of conscience, liberty of trade, and political rights consequent on the ownership of property. In the *Craftsman* he frequently suggests that the first step necessary to preserve these rights is the removal of Walpole from office.

Liberty of trade was the subject of Bolingbroke's series of papers in 1727 dealing with the affairs of the South Sea Company. This great British trading company had returned by this time to more normal functioning after the horrors of the "Bubble" of 1720, when thousands of people had gained and lost fortunes in the madness of speculation. The authors of the *Craftsman* were convinced, as are most historians, that the disaster of the Bubble made Walpole's political career: he was often pictured climbing on the backs of ruined families, consolidating his power at the expense of the unfortunate. The collapse of the South Sea Company in 1720 had assumed the proportions of a national disaster, and for a decade the company continued to be something of a symbol of the nation. This is relevant to Bolingbroke's essays on the company, though these were also designed for narrow political ends. Five of his papers (nos. 60, 61, 62, 65, and 68) appeared during the period leading to the election of the City of London's Court of Aldermen, an oligarchy of twenty-five men "who were generally rich and representative of the financial interests of the great companies."[9]

Writing in no. 60 (26 August 1727) as "Civicus," who states first that he is a "Proprietor in some of the publick Funds; particularly, in the two great *Trading Companys*" (the South Sea and the East India), Bolingbroke poses a set of twenty-four queries about the management of the South Sea Company. Civicus's motive is that he is not "allowed the liberty of inspecting the Accounts and Transactions of *Those*, who are in the *Direction*" (V, 22–23): it is at once obvious that he seeks to expose information that is at present concealed. The questions are rhetorical. Civicus wants to know, for instance, "For *whose Account* those vast sums were *insured* on the *Royal George* [one of the company's ships] outward, as well as homeward bound, which amounted to as much in value, if not more, than what the *Company* had on Board?" (V, 23). The reader does not need to supply the answer, only to note that some persons are using company ships to transport personal goods. The answer is, in fact, suggested by the next query: "Whether it be not a breach of Trust in a *Director* to be concern'd, directly or indirectly, in any *Trade* or *Shipping*, which interferes with the Interest of the Company?" (V, 23). And a further refinement is added as Civicus's tone hardens, and he refers explicitly to "the misconduct of the *Directors*, their *Agents* or *Servants*" (V, 23). Any thought that these are innocent queries must have been dispelled when Civicus's ninth query (the last in no. 60) directly links the fraud he alleges with the forthcoming election: "Whether any Person, who is *known* to be *principally* concern'd in any *Frauds* or *Collusions* of this nature, can be thought a proper Person to be intrusted with the *Rights* and *Privileges* of one of the greatest *trading Cities* in the Universe?" (V, 24). Clearly, these are questions in form only, suggesting openly that the men—directors and their cronies—who conceal the accounts defraud the company for personal gain. The sequence continues in no. 61 (2 September 1727), which Civicus begins by noticing that his first nine queries have not been answered, "from whence the truth of the Facts seem [*sic*] to be tacitly acknowledged" (V, 24).

Further queries follow: should anyone be a governor, sub-governor, or director for above six years; is a man "qualified to be a *Director* of the greatest Company in the Universe, who is unacquainted with *Trade*, and consequently incapable of promoting its true Interest? And what were the Recommendations of *some Persons* to so considerable a Trust?" (V, 24). Can a directorship be so attractive at only £150 per year? "If not, what are the *views*, which occasion such a struggle to get into the *Direction*, since they cannot acquire more, with *Justice to the Company*?" (V, 24). The key to these queries is the stress on the "true Interest" of the company, which by the end of no. 61 has become an example of "over-grown *Companies*," a phrase implying excessive power. The "true Interest" of the company gives way to that of "a *Trading Nation*" as a whole. Bolingbroke's rhetorical strategy is to make no specific allegation (but only ask) and to assert no particular facts (but certainly insinuate). As Civicus, the citizen representing the stockholders, Bolingbroke turns the company's affairs into a major issue that affects the national interest as he asks

> Whether all over-grown *Companies* are not prejudicial to and, in some measure, inconsistent with the *Liberties* of a free People, as well as the true Interest of a *Trading Nation*, with regard to the Influence which they have in the *Elections* of Members of Parliament, particularly for this *great* and *honourable City*; and whether it is not become the Interest and Duty of every Man, who is a Lover of his Country, to oppose such *unwarrantable* and *dangerous Practices?* (V, 25)

The third and last set of queries (no. 62, 9 September 1727) prolongs the fiction that they are all "proposed only for the sake of Information" (V, 25). The general point of these is again that private interest governs the movement of cargoes in company ships. It is easy to imagine an indignant stockholder angrily believing that he is being cheated, but Civicus takes the implications further, asking "Whether a *Parliamentary Enquiry* may not once more be absolutely necessary, in order to prevent the fatal Consequences, which may justly be apprehended to the Nation in general, by the Damage which our *Trade, Navigation* and *Woollen Manufacture* may sustain by such *Practices*, as well as by *Monopolies*?" (V, 27). Only because the South Sea Company is practically synonymous with Britain can the last query have any legitimate and logical place in the sequence, for the practices Bolingbroke tries to expose can be found, by implication, elsewhere in the nation. We shall see that Bolingbroke thought trade and industry nothing less than the lifeblood of the nation.

These papers appeal primarily, though not exclusively, to traders, merchants, and stockholders like their supposed author. The election of the Aldermen and the affairs of the company are entangled, but accompanied by the idea that trade has been infiltrated by outsiders looking for personal profit, and that the health of trade has thus been seriously impaired. The whole is worked into the large context of liberty itself.

Soon after writing these, Bolingbroke wrote a letter (in no. 65, 30 September 1727), under the pseudonym of Charles Freeport. The pseudonym is significant, since the author is "the second Son of *Sir Andrew Freeport*, who had the Happiness of being one of the *Spectator's* Club" (V, 28). Charles Freeport is little more than a name, here or in his later appearances, but Bolingbroke evidently wants to establish a connection with the polite, respected *Spectator* and, therefore, with its readership. The subject of this essay ("which has a Right to claim the Countenance and Encouragement of every honest *Briton*" (V, 27) is the Portuguese Assiento Company, a fictitious parallel to the South Sea Company.[10] Exploiting the irony of the early *Craftsman*, Mr. Freeport notes that "As the principal, if not the only View of the *Portuguese*, was to *amass great Riches for their Families*, a Detail of their Proceedings, like so many Foiles, will illustrate the Candour, and Virtue of our *British Directors*" (V, 28). An equivalent to the South Sea Bubble brings "the *utmost Perplexity*, and had like to have overset the *whole Constitution*" (V, 29), and many of the evils noted in Civicus's queries recur here. Civicus had lamented that he could not examine the company accounts; now Freeport uses the fictional "example" as a warning prediction:

> some *Publick-spirited Men* appeared, who were not to be led, by specious Pretences, or artful insinuations, and demanded a *Scrutiny* into their Books and Papers; which was for some time denied; but being more loudly and strenuously insisted upon, they were compel'd to a Compliance by the *Government:* then, and not till then, their *Chicane* and *Sophistry* manifestly appeared in a true light to all the World! The *deluded Proprietors* were amazed and confounded, to find great part of their Wealth *imaginary*, and that the *real value* of their Stock,... [was] at the Discretion of the *Directors* and their *Friends in Power*, who could, at any time, *raise* or *sink* it as they pleased, according as their *own Interest* and *private Designs* required. (V, 30–31)

In the remaining paragraphs, fictional history predicts optimistically the directors' flight, proving that they can be defeated. Mr. Freeport calls for resistance to fraudulent behavior should it ever occur, he adds ironically, in Britain.

The following week (in no. 68, 21 October 1727), Bolingbroke contributed another, less important, essay on the South Sea Company, in which he repeated the essence of the earlier queries and defended their general stance against opponents in the press. In the election of the Court of Aldermen the opposition gained two seats, a cause for modest celebration, duly expressed on 28 October in no. 69. In no. 71 (11 November 1727) Bolingbroke, writing again as Charles Freeport, resumed the theme that private interest destroys the South Sea Company and even the nation: the "*original Plan*" of the company has been "perverted," and has thus caused

> numberless Evils to the *Proprietors of the Stock*, as well as to the *Nation*: Yet, for this, *Arts* and *Sciences* seem to have been discouraged; *Trade* and *Navigation* neglected; and consequently, the *Exports* of our *Manufactures* are greatly diminished; and what have we got substituted in their room? *Stock Jobbing* . . . together with *Chimerical Schemes*, calculated only to cover and promote . . . the *sinister Designs* of a set of Men, who, like Cankers, preyed on the Vitals of their Country, till they had reduced it to the lowest and most declining Condition. (V, 34–35)

The discussion that follows exposes the company's failure to be profitable to its stockholders or to the nation as a whole, the importance of which finally becomes apparent as Bolingbroke expresses his fundamental assumption about trade:

> It is *freedom* of *Trade*, which is the Spring of Riches, and the Animal Spirits of any Nation; and as we have happily experienced this undoubted Truth, by the Figure which we have seen our Country make in the World, so we may be assured, while we pursue contrary Measures, that we shall decline in *Strength* and *Power*, the natural Consequences of *Riches*. It was *Trade* that enabled us to spend so many *Millions* in defence of our *Rights* and *Liberties*; and therefore, while we are desirous of preserving those inestimable Blessings, we cannot be too vigilant or tender of it. (V, 37–38)

By "perverting" the South Sea Company, these fraudulent men are accused of preying on the "Vitals of their *Country*" (V, 35; my italics); and since trade supports liberty, these men threaten the liberty of the nation itself.

Bolingbroke's next contributions (to nos. 91, 93, and 96) continue the theme that South Sea Company ships are used to carry contraband without the knowledge of the owner. In no. 91 (30 March 1728) Bolingbroke argues that it is unfair to prosecute the owner under the Navigation Act, if such a case of fraud is discovered, and he takes the opportunity at the end of his letter to repeat that "*all our Wealth and Grandeur entirely depend*" on trade (V, 42). His second letter in no. 91 points to yet more mismanagement in the company, and a brief letter (in no. 93, 13 April 1728) reemphasizes his points about the Navigation Act, adding that such illegal imports are "a *growing Evil*" (V, 44). Charles Freeport's letter (in no. 96, 4 May 1728) argues that the company must be "notoriously injured" while "a few *private Persons*" profit; exasperated, he asks "is the *Interest* of the *Company*, or the *Nation* to be thus exposed for any *private, unjust Gain* whatever?" (V, 46).

From the late summer of 1728 until early in 1729, Bolingbroke returned regularly to the subject of trade, but interspersed his essays with two papers on the need for free elections (nos. 111 and 123), occasioned by allegations of corrupt influence on voters in an election in the Welsh borough of Montgomery in May 1728. Of his six essays on trade during this period, one, no. 114 (7 September 1728), is particularly important.[11] Here Bolingbroke expresses his creed on the subject, bringing together most of his theoretical ideas and historical examples into a single, coherent statement of the vital importance of trade to the nation.

Early in this essay Charles Freeport links trade and liberty, rightly (he says) believed by everyone to be interdependent. Britain, with few natural resources, must rely on trade for her wealth, which will flourish if "all the Subjects of *England*" are allowed, or rather, encouraged, to participate: the more traders, the greater the exports, "and consequently all *exclusive Companies* are generally allowed to be *prejudicial* to the Nation" (V, 54–55). One present example of such a monopoly (compared with past examples of declining British trade in various parts of the world) is the South Sea Company, which trades "beyond [its] *Limits*" and can therefore "make *all other Traders* and *Manufacturers*, and almost *every Corporation* in *England* dependent" on the company (V, 56). Such dependence will menace the constitution, trade, and liberty, and thus diminish British power. But there is worse yet to come. No sooner does a company receive a monopolistic charter than immediately arises a Sett of Men called *Governours, Sub-Governours, Directors, Stock-Jobbers*, &c. who divide their Stock into *Shares*, and then negotiate them in the *Alley*, before it is known whether they have any *intrinsick Value* or not; and if there be any *true Value*, which few of them ever had, instead of carrying on the Design by *fair and industrious Means*, some wicked *Artifice* is contrived to raise it to an *imaginary Heighth*, and thereby delude and ruin many Thousands of innocent and unwary Persons. (V, 57)

By raising the specter of delusion and ruin, Bolingbroke means to remind his readers of the horror of the South Sea Bubble; once more, he suggests, a clique of individuals can bring disaster to the entire nation. Further, as in 1720, some of these "Villains of the deepest Dye who, in effect, rob the Fatherless and Widows, in common with thousands of others, usually escape with Impunity" (V, 57). Not only is the trade unfair and the price of the stocks manipulated by men in the know, but the accounts do not even have to be published. The result of all this is not merely the decline of the company:

Hath not *Trade* decay'd ever since *Stock-jobbing* flourished and met with encouragement? have not our *Manufacturies* diminished, our *Imports* and *Exports* in general declined, and our *Poor* become more numerous for want of Employ? are not his Majesty's *Customs* impaired, and will they not waste still more and more proportionably with our *Trade*?

In fine, to what dangerous uses may these *Companies* be made subservient, by *corrupt* and *enterprizing Ministers?* Is it not in their Power to conceal any *Advices* from Abroad, which may affect our *Stocks*, till they have *bought* or *sold out*; and may they not, at any other time, raise or fall them at their Pleasure? (V, 57–58)

In these rhetorical questions governors of the company have been casually replaced by ministers of state. Bolingbroke at last makes it clear that the men presiding over the new ruin of the company and of the nation are men in national government. Inextricably intertwined, politics and finance produce corruption and ruin. The significance of Bolingbroke's essays on corrupt influence at elections now emerges: "Have not all *Ministries* an influence over those *Companies*, and may they not by their means be able to *influence* the *Elections* of every City, and *Trading Town* in *England*?" This "formidable, complicated Power" therefore threatens the constitution (V, 58). Since Bolingbroke has linked the mismanagement of the South

Sea Company with the state of the nation, the closing paragraph of no. 114 resounds with irony: "We are indeed secure under the *present Administration*, who have given such demonstrations of their virtue and disinterested love of their Country, that they can never be suspected of any *corrupt or dangerous Practices*" (V, 58).

Late in 1728 Bolingbroke began to share conspicuously with his fellow authors the ironical device of discussing the hypothetical or general case of (for instance) "an evil minister." In no. 123 (9 November 1728) he satirizes Walpole without specifically naming him, under such terms as "some *wicked Minister*," "*despotic, evil Ministers*," "*Great Men*," "a *base Minister* [who] has, by a foul and wicked Administration, drawn upon him the Odium and Resentment of the People," "a *guilty, hated Minister*," an imaginary minister who, "thro' *Incapacity* or *Ignorance, Pride*, or *Insolence*, should offend some *foreign Power*," a "*corrupt*" and "*over grown*" and "*wicked Minister*." After this catalog Bolingbroke, with customary irony, feels he "must now congratulate my Country, that this is not our Case at present" (V, 59–63).

The rhetoric of this essay, which obviously invites the satirical comparison with Walpole, foreshadows the method of satire through historical example that Bolingbroke would use nearly two years later in the *Remarks on the History of England*. This method, already used earlier in the *Craftsman*, is itself discussed in no. 142 (22 March 1729) as a cause of "Offence or Uneasiness" to the opponents of Mr. D'Anvers. The ironic purpose of the essay, however, is to introduce a parallel between Walpole and the Dutch statesman Johan de Witt. Bolingbroke surprisingly gives no prominence to the system of patronage upon which de Witt's entire machinery of power depended. Instead, he concentrates on de Witt's correspondence with members of the French court to prove that the Dutchman placed his country at risk. Although not exact, the intended parallel with Walpole was provocative, since, says Bolingbroke, de Witt's treasonable activity remained unpunished. But the paper finally warns Walpole that he may meet the same grisly fate as de Witt and his brother.[12]

Bolingbroke's next ten contributions reveal less thematic unity than his essays on trade, but most contain some attack on Walpole's corrupt system of selling offices in government. Two papers make use of the "example" again: in one attack Bolingbroke quotes a speech by Charles Sedley in support of William III against private interest (no. 147, 26 April 1729) and in another he discusses the case of the notoriously barbarous keeper of the Fleet Prison, Thomas Bambridge (no. 149, 10 May 1729).

This essay was prompted by a House of Commons Committee report on the state of the Fleet, declaring that Bambridge

> hath wilfully permitted several debtors of the crown in great sums of money, as well as debtors to divers of his majesty's subjects, to escape; hath been guilty of the most notorious breaches of his trust, great extortions, and the highest crimes and misdemeanours in the execution of his said office: and hath arbitrarily and unlawfully loaded with irons, put into dungeons, and destroyed prisoners for debt, under his charge, treating them in the most barbarous and cruel manner, in high violation and contempt of the laws of this kingdom.[13]

To Bolingbroke and his coadjutors, these strong words must have looked like a condemnation of the minister himself, but Bolingbroke makes less than he might out of possible parallels between the jailer and the minister. True, Bambridge and his confederates are described as "Him and his Chief Ministers," and, like Walpole in numerous *Craftsman* essays, Bambridge "seems to be well experienc'd, and improv'd, in the Management and Disposition of *Publick Accounts* and *Revenues*" (V, 91, 93). But despite such parallels, the main purpose of the essay appears to be less to satirize Walpole than to offer an outraged comment on the notorious Bambridge scandal.

Bolingbroke's essay in no. 154 (14 June 1729) enquires "by what Marks a good Minister may be found out and distinguished" and contrasts truly public-spirited men who enter politics with the corrupt ministers they meet.[14] In no. 161 (2 August 1729) Bolingbroke exposes luxury, extravagance, and corruption, dwelling upon "the greatest *Political* Evil [which] is *Venality of Offices*; because . . . This is generally attended with *Corruption* in Office; which is the original Source, from whence all other *political Evils* may be properly said to flow" (V, 96). Both these papers use the rhetorical device of stating a general case and—by means of irony—suggesting a specific application. On 13 September 1729, no. 167 contained a strange and uncharacteristic letter on dogs which implies parallels between certain patterns of behavior among dogs and bribed men. Bolingbroke's next contribution (no. 181, 20 December 1729) was occasional, celebrating the recent acquittal of Richard Francklin, who had been on trial for printing a seditious libel in the *Craftsman.*

After the Treaty of Seville was formally concluded on 9 November 1729, Bolingbroke turned briefly to foreign affairs. In no. 185 (17 January 1730) he uses the treaty to lead to the common complaints about "*Foreign Forces* in *English Pay*" (V, 107). Although his next contribution (to no. 186, 24 January 1730), merely repeats this theme, these essays are followed by one of greater interest and scope, no. 199 (25 April 1730), in which he assesses the settlement of Seville.

In June he began his series on history, which ran for nearly a year. While this series was appearing, he made only three other contributions. One was a collaborative effort (no. 225, 24 October 1730) in which Bolingbroke and Amhurst defended the cursory treatment of the reign of Henry VI in the *Remarks on the History of England.* The second was an insignificant verse in no. 249 (10 April 1731). And the third was the text (in no. 252, 1 May 1731) of the Monumental Inscription at Blenheim Palace.[15]

Remarks on the History of England

On 13 June 1730 the *Craftsman*, no. 206, contained a letter from "Humphrey Oldcastle," who recounted a conversation in a coffeehouse. This was the first of Oldcastle's twenty-four letters to Caleb D'Anvers, in which Bolingbroke discussed the history of England from the Norman conquest to the reign of Charles I. By 22 May 1731, when the series ended, the *London Journal, Daily Courant*, and *Flying Post* had condemned several of the letters, Francklin had been arrested for printing two of them, and Bolingbroke had initiated a debate about historiography that was to last ten years. More immediately, his last letter, in which he defended his own and Pulteney's earlier conduct, provoked a pamphlet war of several months, involving much abuse but little genuine achievement. As Bolingbroke said, he had provoked "volumes of scurrility."[16]

The *Remarks* caused a furor and brought the *Craftsman* to yet greater popularity, though it may now be difficult to understand why. The long sequence of essays characterizes English history as a perpetual struggle between the spirit of faction and the spirit of liberty, and analyzes the policy and conduct of successive monarchs. The avowed purpose of the essays is to help revive the spirit of liberty and restore the British constitution. Oldcastle expects to extirpate partisan or private interest and thus revive true concern for the national interest. Walpole quickly set his journalists to the task of opposing Bolingbroke because it was apparent that Mr. Oldcastle was going to "prove" that England was, in 1730, a slave to private interest. The essays also coherently suggest that the ideal constitution should be represented by a perfect balance between king, lords, and commons and that the "spirit of faction" tries to upset or destroy that balance. Liberty means good, faction means evil. Although such a subject might seem too theoretical or philosophical to catch the popular imagination, the essays contain a rhetorical element that undoubtedly contributed to their popularity.

The *Remarks* begin with three largely introductory letters.[17] Bolingbroke places all discussion on the level of a coffeehouse debate and also indicates that the *Craftsman* itself is "chiefly answerable" for a new spirit of political enquiry among "All orders of men." In the first essay the company of gentlemen whose conversation is to be related "often meets, rather to live than to drink together; . . . They dispute without strife, and examine as dispassionately the events and the characters of the present age, as they reason about those which are found in history" (292). Clearly, Bolingbroke portrays the gentlemen as sober and reasonable; thus, their deliberations and judgments seem sober and reasonable. All agree that if Mr. D'Anvers's papers "could be suspected to be written in opposition to the present ministers, the feeble and low opposition you have met with would deserve to be looked upon as a very melancholy symptom for them, since it would denote that their cause was deemed universally bad, or that their persons were grown universally odious among men of sense, ingenuity, and knowledge. It would denote their guilt, or their misfortune; perhaps both" (293). The public, they determine, has "a right to be informed, and to reason about public affairs." And

when wise and honest measures are pursued, and the nation reaps the advantage of them, the exercise of this right will always be agreeable to the men in power; that, indeed, if weak and wicked measures are pursued, the men in power might find the exercise of this right disagreeable, inconvenient, and sometimes dangerous to them; but that, even in this case, there would be no pretence for attempting to deprive the people of this right, or for discouraging the exercise of it: and that to forbid men to complain, when they suffer, would be an instance of tyranny but one degree below that which the triumvirs gave, during the slaughter and terror of the proscriptions, when by edict they commanded all men to be merry upon pain of death. (293)

The cumulative irony of these passages, which summarize the judgments of these worthy gentlemen, indicates that the *Craftsman* has been (as none of its regular readers would really need to be told) resisting a weak and wicked administration for four years. One "ancient venerable gentleman" (294) adds his voice, saying that the *Craftsman* "has contributed to raise" (295) a certain spirit in the nation—neither Whiggism nor Toryism, but a mixture, appealing to members of both parties, which it "would be too absurd" to call Jacobitism (295). With emphasis on national—not party—concerns, Bolingbroke suggests that this spirit is "a revival of the true old English spirit, which prevailed in the days of our fathers, and which must always be national, since it has no direction but to the national interest" (295). This is what will become identified with the "spirit of liberty."

The first essay is important because it establishes all the rhetorical connections. Liberty itself, "a tender plant" that must be "cultivated with incessant care" (296), is associated with the *Craftsman*. The discussion of the general political situation in 1730, as compared with that in 1726, when the *Craftsman* began, is undertaken by people whose testimony is shown to be reliable. They conclude that the *Craftsman* valuably promotes—or defends—the cause of liberty in the face of an evil government. Liberty, says the old man, can be in danger under any sort of government, and in particular "is it more exposed under limited monarchies than under any other form of mixed government" (298) because a king has so much power. The first essay leaves no doubt that liberty is threatened by Walpole's corrupt administration.

In the second essay Bolingbroke adds that the spirit of liberty works slowly, but effectually, and that the loss of the spirit of liberty leads to the loss of liberty itself. Citing the example of Rome's decline under its monstrous emperors, he tells us authoritatively: "We must not imagine that the freedom of the Romans was lost, because one party fought for the maintenance of liberty; another for the establishment of tyranny; and that the latter prevailed. No. The spirit of liberty was dead, and the spirit of faction had taken its place on both sides" (304). When the spirit of liberty prevailed, personal interest was sacrificed to the interest of the commonwealth; but when faction prevailed, personal interests dominated national concerns, and the result was slavery. As in his first essay, Bolingbroke argues again for a balanced constitution, and again dissociates himself from Jacobitism, this time by conspicuously disapproving of the Jacobite paper, *Fog's Weekly Journal.* In the first two essays he carefully lays the foundations for the whole series, including a distinction that identifies one of his principal targets: "A spirit of liberty will be always and wholly concerned about national interests, and very indifferent about personal and private interests. On the contrary, a spirit of faction will be always and wholly concerned about these, and very indifferent about the others. When they appear, therefore, in their proper characters, they are distinguished as easily as light and darkness; and the danger I apprehend is over" (305–6). After Bolingbroke's repeated essays on trade, liberty, the South Sea Company, and the men who act dishonestly for private gain, there is no doubt that Walpole, by encouraging a spirit of faction, threatens the liberty of the nation.

These first two letters provoked immediate responses in the *London Journal* and the *Daily Courant.* Bolingbroke's third essay retorts by trying to silence these opponents in the press. He uses a straightforward argument with an utterly authoritative tone. Appealing continually to the authority of facts, he dismisses the author of the *London Journal* as "this able person" (313) who knows "as little of Livy as he does of Machiavel, or," he adds with contempt, "I believe of any other good author. . . . He succeeds, you see, but ill, when he meddles with facts; and I do not find that he pretends to much reason" (314). Oldcastle troubles to answer a journalist only, perhaps, because to do so places his own command of history—but, most important, of the "facts"—in a position of eminence. The narrator of the series emerges from this paper as perfectly reliable.

The series of essays on individual portions of history opens with letter 4, which discusses the Normans, with the emphasis at once placed upon the indomitable spirit of liberty. Even so apparently absolute a monarch as William I, says Mr. Oldcastle, could not destroy the English constitution. In a pattern that becomes familiar throughout the series, Bolingbroke appeals to the Englishman's reverence for the past and for what might be called traditional values and rights. In the fifth letter he illustrates his contention that the spirit of liberty is slow but effectual by referring to the reigns of Edward III, Richard II, and Henry IV. Bolingbroke also introduces an obvious warning by noting that Edward III was great and good—even to the extent of removing a son and a favorite mistress from the court in the interests of the nation. At the end of the essay Bolingbroke introduces a general example in contrast to Edward III:

A prince, who adds to the national stock, has a right to share the advantage he procures, and may demand supplies from his people without blushing. But a prince, who lives a rent-charge on the nation he governs, who sits on the throne, like a monstrous drone in the middle of a hive, draining all the combs of their honey, and neither making nor assisting the industrious bees to make any; such a prince, I say, ought to blush at every grant he receives from a people, who never received any benefit from him. The Duke of Gloucester told Richard the Second, on his restoring Brest to the Duke of Brittany, that he should have taken a town by his own valor and conduct, before he resigned what his ancestors had left him. Much to the same purpose might an oppressed people justly answer a craving prince. When you have increased the riches and advanced the prosperity of the nation, you will have some right to make these demands upon us; but till then we shall think that you have none. (324)

Since 1726 Bolingbroke had been explaining in the *Craftsman* that English trade was in decay, the national debt increasing, and national prosperity being retarded. Here, Richard II is only an analogue of the general case, not an exact example of a "craving prince." Bolingbroke, in fact, names no specific king, but suggests that the English people are oppressed and that their king may, with justice, be paralleled by such a general example. The "example" formula thus hints at adverse criticism of George II. The *Craftsman*'s printer was promptly arrested for printing this paper.

Bolingbroke's sixth letter was, if anything, even more outspoken in its criticism of both George and Walpole. Among the articles "setting forth the particulars of [Richard II's] misgovernment" were two which Bolingbroke quoted: "That he had put the administration of the public affairs in the hands of unexperienced and ill-designing persons, to the great damage of the people, who were loaded with excessive taxes. That in his negotiations with foreign princes, he had made use of so many equivocations and sophistries, that none would take his word any more" (328). The authors of ripostes in the *Flying Post* and the *London Journal* unwisely accused Mr. Oldcastle of having invented these quotations in order to suggest a parallel. It must have been satisfying for Bolingbroke that his opponents did the work of applying the parallel. With considerable glee, Amhurst replied that these were of course genuine quotations (and he gave volume and page references to the books they came from), adding that he hoped that these writers would not "pretend to reason upon *History*, before they read it" (no. 219, 12 September 1730). Francklin was arrested for printing this paper, too.

Yet one arrest made Caleb D'Anvers more, not less, defiant:

> *Notwithstanding the Exceptions that have been taken to our former* Remarks, *and which have drawn some uncommon Proceedings upon Mr.* Francklin, *we are determined to prosecute our Design, and humbly apprehend that any* Englishman *hath a Privilege (as long as the* Liberty of the Press *continues) to give the Publick an* Abstract of the English History, *and to make such* Observations *upon it, as naturally result from it. As for Mr.* Oldcastle *and* my self, *we shall always take particular Care not to assert any Thing in the Course of these* Remarks, *but what we can justify by undoubted Authority from the* best Historians. (no. 219, 12 September 1730)

It must have been obvious to Walpole that Bolingbroke was defying him to prosecute. The seventh letter discusses the demise of Richard II, but laments that it was faction that removed him and encouraged Henry IV to act illegally and tyrannically. Bolingbroke then discusses the Wars of the Roses, in which "The national interest was sunk, to the shame of the nation, in the particular interest of two families" (330). The central portion of this essay discusses one, specific consequence of the "watchful spirit of liberty" (331): laws, still in operation in 1730, designed to prevent corrupt influence on voters at the election of members of Parliament. Free elections are, simply, the basis of English freedom: to lose it is to be left "at the mercy of any ambitious prince, or wicked minister" (331). Once again, the effect of four years of *Craftsman* papers that had alleged corrupt influence at elections, and had alleged that the national interest was "sunk" in the particular interest of Walpole and his family, must suggest that these remarks are intended as a commentary on the present. The British constitution must need urgent attention. Bolingbroke becomes still more defiant when he declares that he will oppose the author of the *London Journal* "without the least fear of being crush'd by the weight of his arguments; or, which is more, by the power of his patron" (331). The challenge to Walpole could not have been more evident.

At this point in the essay Bolingbroke changes direction and begins to answer the *London Journal*, then attacks the entire band of Walpole's journalists: "To screen their patrons, they endeavor to distinguish us out of our greatest national advantages . . . to reconcile the minds of men to such measures as their patrons may want, and as no honest man will take, they endeavor to demolish the very corner stones on which the whole fabric of liberty rests" (334). Their doctrines are as destructive of liberty as those of Archbishop Laud, whose assault on liberty was open, but Walpole's men "are privately poisoning the root of liberty" (334). Bolingbroke explains that he has dwelt upon the writings of Walpole's journalists "to shew what is the real design of these remarks" (335): anyone opposing the published doctrine of the ministry will be seen "to be the truest friends to his majesty king George, and the Protestant succession" (335).

The battle in the press was important. The press provided Bolingbroke's only personal opportunity to express his opposition, and Walpole subsidized several journals in an attempt to stop the flood of criticism of him in the *Craftsman.* In the weeks when the *Craftsman* did not contain an essay from the *Remarks*, Amhurst devoted considerable space to arguments in favor of the liberty of the press, in the context of the series on history. These papers raised the vexed questions of interpretation, of what constituted innuendo, and of when an historical parallel could be deemed libelous.[18] Just as the authors and the printer of the *Craftsman* had good experience to help them through their legal difficulties, so in Bolingbroke they had a writer with the historical facts of his series at his command. As soon as the eighth letter had been published, condemning Edward IV's queen, Elizabeth Woodville, for filling the court with her own favorites and exiling those who were not, the *Daily Courant* accused Bolingbroke of passing too superficially over the reign of Henry VI. In no. 225 (24 October 1730) Bolingbroke and Amhurst readily obliged with a lengthy reply answering every material point, and adding further satirical parallels.

Perhaps the most obviously applicable of all Bolingbroke's examples is that of Cardinal Wolsey in the tenth letter. The origin of all England's troubles in Henry VIII's reign "lay in the private interests and passions of Wolsey, . . . If Henry the Eighth negotiated perpetually, and was perpetually the bubble of those with whom and for whom he negotiated, this happened chiefly because he was, in the first place, the bubble of his minister" (348). Wolsey was avaricious and ambitious, and every contemporary knew he was an analogue of Walpole, since the parallel had been used, in different words, in nine earlier issues of the *Craftsman.*[19] By implication perhaps, George II might be seen in the figure of Henry VIII who, under Wolsey's influence, becomes in Bolingbroke's judgment the worst, the most evil, of all the monarchs he discusses.

By now, Walpole was casting about for any reason at all to arrest the printer, or in some other way to stop the *Craftsman.* In January 1731 he did find a reason, but it had nothing to do with the *Remarks.* Using information from one of Bolingbroke's European contacts, no. 235 exposed Walpole's shabby foreign negotiations. Seriously embarrassed, Walpole had Francklin arrested. Helped by the Juries Act, which enabled Walpole to fill a jury in Westminster with citizens of his own political persuasion, the minister got his revenge for Francklin's acquittal two years before. Francklin was imprisoned for a year and fined heavily, but the effect of his sentence was to make him a martyr and thereby raise the circulation of the *Craftsman.* Three weeks earlier Bolingbroke's twelfth letter had been published, and in it he recognized that, now his essays were getting nearer to modern times, "it is probable that they will become the occasions of louder complaints, and of more impertinent clamor" (357). This he will regret because the violent reaction against his efforts to revive the spirit of liberty—"in a country where liberty is still avowed"—has already been "most suspicious and melancholy" (357).

Having established that the most tyrannical ruler was Henry VIII, Bolingbroke wrote in his next four letters (thirteen to sixteen) about the opposite kind of reign, in which the spirit of liberty was encouraged by the monarch. This was the golden age of England, the reign of Elizabeth. Bolingbroke dwells on the affection of the people for Elizabeth, on her moderation, openness, frugality, caution in foreign negotiations, and belief that the crown should neither hoard nor lavish the people's money. One contemporary application, for Bolingbroke, linked trade and liberty in his favorite way. For about a century and a half, since Elizabeth's encouragement,

> Commerce has thrived under neglects and discouragement. It has subsisted under oppressions and obstructions; and the spirit of it is not yet extinguished by that of stockjobbing; though the spirit of stockjobbing be to that of trade, what the spirit of faction is to that of liberty. The tendency of both is to advance the interest of a few worthless individuals, at the expense of the whole community. The consequence of both, if ever they prevail to the ruin of trade and liberty, must be, that the harpies will starve in the midst of imaginary wealth; and that the children of faction, like the iron race of Cadmus, will destroy one another. (375–76)

This is, of course, partisan history.

The next seven essays examine the deplorable state of the nation under James I and Charles I, both of them parallels of George II. Among the satirical implications that refer to earlier issues of the *Craftsman* are Bolingbroke's insistence that liberty is preserved through the independence of Parliament and his account of James's profuse squandering. Once again, Walpole too can be recognized in the generalized portrait: "The immense estates, which were made in these days at court, the known corruption not only of inferior agents, but of principal ministers, and even of those who were at the head of the treasury, made such an examination [of the king's finances] the more necessary, and provoked and excited the more to it" (424). The *Craftsman* had been clamoring for years to have public accounts made public. Walpole's "immense estates," his bribery of "inferior agents," his "known corruption . . . at the head of the treasury" were all common, well-known allegations in the *Craftsman.* And by speaking of such things occurring "in these days," Bolingbroke insinuates a reference to the present, whereas "those days" (the more expected phrase) would unambiguously refer to the past he purports to be discussing.

The purpose of all these essays is not merely to suggest that George is a weak or wicked king, or Walpole a weak or wicked minister, but also to emphasize the disastrous consequences of failing to recognize the decline of the nation. It is no use thinking that Britain is prosperous and free. On the contrary, Bolingbroke seeks to expose the "truth" that, despite appearances, Britain is neither particularly prosperous nor genuinely free. History shows how faction can be resisted, how the constitution can be preserved, and therefore how liberty can be maintained. In the most controversial paper of the whole series Bolingbroke looks back on the sequence he is winding up in no. 255.

First Bolingbroke considers how "so great an alarm was taken at the first direct avowal of an attempt to revive the spirit of liberty, and to recall to the minds of men the true notions of the British constitution" (447). He calls the press response to the *Remarks* a campaign undertaken by a swarm of insects, from which he has been mercifully free by retiring to the country. The "real crime," he points out, has not been his manner of treating the subject, but treating it at all. The earliest letters, he says, caused a storm of protest from Walpole's writers, yet the letters contain nothing but general and inoffensive reflections: "this new alarm was taken, . . . at the general design of those papers; and if that was sufficient to give such an alarm, sure I am that you [Caleb D'Anvers] are more than justified for all you wrote before this dispute begun, and for all you have published in the course of it" (448). It is now clear, he says, that "a contrary spirit" to that of liberty "hath been raised, and that principles, destructive of all liberty, and particularly adapted to destroy that of the British government, are avowed, taught, and propagated . . . Nothing less, therefore, than a constant and vigorous opposition, of which you have set us the example, will be able to stop the progress of those pernicious doctrines" (448–49). The first part of this letter argues that press resistance to the *Remarks* confirms Bolingbroke's fear that Walpole's government threatens to extinguish liberty. The first part ends with a rhetorical flourish that brings the *Craftsman* to the close of its first four years of prominence: Bolingbroke hopes that Caleb D'Anvers "will succeed in the cause you have undertaken—the cause of your country, the cause of truth and of liberty" (450). Those who belong to the cause are many, "who have not bowed the knee to Baal, nor worshipped the brazen image" (451). The biblical echoes suggest resistance and faith, but since the "brazen image" refers to Walpole's nickname "brazen face," it is obvious who needs to be resisted.

The second part of this final essay defends Bolingbroke and Pulteney, but opens by warning Walpole that he should "tremble at a clamor which he knows ought, and which he hath reason to fear will, sooner or later, prevail against him" (451–52). Against the charge that Pulteney "hath left his friends and party, and that he is urged to oppose the minister by the stings of disappointed ambition," (452) Bolingbroke answers with a string of rhetorical questions designed to prove that the charge is ridiculous. He then considers his own case, denying the charge of ingratitude to Marlborough and Godolphin. He acknowledges the clemency of George I in pardoning him, but the king's intentions were not fulfilled, "due solely to the minister['s] ambition, his groundless jealousy and private interest" (454). Bolingbroke finally asserts that his connection with the Pretender ceased when he was dismissed. It was perhaps precisely because Bolingbroke dropped the rhetorical mask of Oldcastle and returned to direct self-justification that this essay—particularly this part of it—roused so much counter-criticism.

The *Remarks* approach a form of *controversiae* with modernized applications that continually angered Walpole and his writers. The whole method of satire by historical parallel had been carefully introduced and attention drawn to it; in fact, many of the specific local points in the history had already been made in previous issues of the *Craftsman*. With his audience primed, Bolingbroke put together a sequence of articles certain to be recognized as political satire. Once the immediate controversy was over, the general tendency was to read the *Remarks* as a discussion of the British constitution, primarily, and not as a satire. If the *Remarks* appear to demonstrate Britain's ills, Bolingbroke's other major work of this period, *A Dissertation upon Parties*, seems to offer an alternative.

A Dissertation upon Parties

One of the selling points of *A Dissertation upon Parties* was its belligerent dedication "To the Right Honourable Sir Robert Walpole." The "Famous Dedication" was even reprinted separately, becoming in some ways a symbol of Bolingbroke's most outspoken challenge to Walpole. The *Dissertation* was the most frequently reprinted of all Bolingbroke's works: indeed after its appearance in nineteen letters in the *Craftsman* between 27 October 1733 and 21 December 1734, it was reprinted in book form twice in quick succession at Francklin's shop. This important work, as Caleb D'Anvers proudly noted in 1737, had received "so much Applause, that it stands in Need of no Recommendation."[20] Swift told Pope that the *Dissertation* was "masterly written," and Bolingbroke himself was proud of it.[21]

That the *Dissertation* first appeared in the *Craftsman* suggests that it might contain more of Bolingbroke's satirical and rhetorical technique. Bolingbroke states in his dedication that "these little essays" are designed to

> expose the artifice, and to point out the series of misfortunes, by which we were divided formerly into parties, whose contests brought even the fundamental principles of our constitution into question, and whose excesses brought liberty to the very brink of ruin.

They are also designed "to revive in the minds of men the true spirit" of the British constitution, and to vindicate the advantages of the revolution settlement of 1688. Importantly, Bolingbroke sets out "to unite men of all denominations" at the expense of party distinctions, in order to perpetuate those advantages.[22] These ends, he insists, can have nothing to do with Jacobitism, nor can they be a cause of shame or fear: "No; they are designs in favor of the constitution; designs to secure, to fortify, to perpetuate that excellent system of government. I court no other cause; I claim no other merit" (6). Bolingbroke indicates how far the *Craftsman* has succeeded in bringing public affairs into the domain of every man's interest. Every man in 1735 would agree that "the British constitution is the business of every Briton" and the particular business of Walpole, since he is answerable for the government (7). By using a contrasting pair of examples, Bolingbroke accuses Walpole of governing "ignorantly, weakly, [and] even wickedly" (7) and of willingness to "connive at such indirect violations of the rules of the constitution as tend to the destruction of it, or even at such evasions as tend to render it useless" (8).

Bolingbroke explains that party divisions can be only factious if the national interest is the genuine desire of all men. He accuses Walpole of keeping alive the pretense of party divisions only to prevent unity from threatening his own power. The "hypothetical" minister who protects himself this way governs by faction: "He must of course select a faction to himself; and this faction must be composed, to answer his purposes, of men servilely obsequious, or extremely inferior to him by their talents. Whenever this happens, the reign of venality, of prostitution, of ignorance, of futility, and of dulness commences" (13). Again, Bolingbroke discusses Walpole's apologists. In contrast to Bolingbroke himself and the *Craftsman*, which defends "The cause of the British constitution" (15), Walpole and his newspapers "labor . . . to make [Walpole's] preservation and the destruction of the constitution a common cause" (16). Bolingbroke observes that a *personal* altercation between himself and Walpole is of no public interest (18), and he therefore keeps to public subjects, while by contrast Walpole's writers conduct a campaign of personal denigration against Bolingbroke. Bolingbroke's rhetoric establishes himself as an impartial friend to liberty, standing above the level of petty malice and squabbling and concerned only with what is good for the public.

A Dissertation upon Parties was not, it seems, originally intended to run to nineteen essays. The first eleven essays were published in the *Craftsman* over a period of fourteen weeks. The ninth essay hints that the series is drawing to a close; the eleventh announces the closure. Ten months later, in November 1734, Bolingbroke returned to the series, adding eight essays, the last of which surveys the others. The form of the series is once again epistolary, but as with the *Remarks,* the form is often token: little critical emphasis can be placed on "letters" that are obviously portions of a continuous essay, with "Sir" before them and "I am, Sir, Yours &c" at the end. The *Dissertation* is continuous, not a set of related but independent essays, like the *Remarks*; but in places the *Dissertation* does share the satiric method of the earlier work.

Anyone reading "A spirit of liberty, transmitted down from our Saxon ancestors, and the unknown ages of our government, preserved itself through one almost continual struggle, against the usurpations of our princes, and the vices of our people," (84) might think the sentence came from the *Remarks* and would probably endorse Kramnick's view that the *Dissertation*, "ostensibly a discussion of parties," really continues the *Remarks*.[23] But the *Dissertation* does discuss parties, even if Bolingbroke attaches more weight to the need to preserve the constitution from insidious corruption. Also, in addition to using historical parallels, many of the essays satirize both Walpole and George II by other means.

The method of parallels is established in the second essay: the evil principles of the reigns of James I and Charles I

> were only kept down for a time by worse; and, therefore, they rose again at the restoration, and revived with the monarchy. Thus that epidemical taint, with which king James infected the minds of men, continued upon us: and it is scarce hyperbolical to say, that this prince hath been the original cause of a series of misfortunes to this nation, as deplorable as a lasting infection of our air, of our water, or our earth, would have been. The spirit of his reign was maintained in that of his son, (for how could it well be otherwise, when the same ministers were continued in power?) and the events of both produced the civil war. (30–31)

By saying that a "taint . . . continued upon *us*," Bolingbroke speaks implicitly not only of his ancestors, but of his own generation. Also, the words which gain prominence, and therefore irony, in the original *Craftsman* by being printed in italics include the sequence of "*this Prince*," "his *Son*," and "the same *Ministers*." It requires little imagination to identify, respectively, George I, George II, and Walpole. Further than this identification, no exact correspondence is possible, but

Bolingbroke surely intends a general parallel, as another warning that parallel disasters may occur—or are occurring—in the 1730s. Similarly, Charles II's corrupt "pensioner parliament" (40) is a parallel forerunner of the Parliament of 1733:

> ... in the case now before us, we have a very comfortable example of a court wicked enough to stand in need of corruption, and to employ it; and a parliament virtuous enough to resist the force of this expedient, ... (40–41)

Bribery is necessary only if the court acts against the public interest. But Bolingbroke speaks of "the case now before us." Which case? the present or the past? Bolingbroke does mean the past, but he insinuates an association with the present, which he allows to remain ambiguous in the reader's mind for a short time first.

Repeating a sequence of conditionals is also one of his methods of suggesting a parallel or, here, something rather more than a parallel:

> If king Charles had found the nation plunged in corruption; the people choosing their representatives for money, without any other regard; and these representatives of the people, as well as the nobility, reduced by luxury to beg the unhallowed alms of a court; or to receive, like miserable hirelings, the wages of iniquity from a minister: if he had found the nation, I say, in this condition, (which extravagant supposition one cannot make without horror) he might have dishonored her abroad, and impoverished and oppressed her at home, ... (63)

If all these conditions had prevailed, Charles would have presided over "the very quintessence of political misery" (63). The rhetorical accumulation suggests another, implicit statement to be added when Bolingbroke says, "But this was not the state of the English nation, at the time we speak of. We were not yet corrupted, nor even quite ripe for corruption" (63). No, but such *is* the state of the English nation now; we *are* corrupted now.

Bolingbroke employs a similar technique in the fourteenth letter. Discussing the Spanish constitution under Charles V, he digresses to a general observation:

> In aristocracies, the nobility get whatever the commons lose; but in monarchies, the crown alone is the gainer, and the certain consequence of their

helping to enslave the commons, must be that of being enslaved themselves at last. How indeed, should it be otherwise, since the liberty of the commons cannot be taken away unless the constitution be first broken; and since neither the peers, nor any one else, can hold their privileges or their properties, by a better tenure than that of arbitrary will, when the constitution is once broken? Was it possible to doubt this truth, we might find the proof of it, without going out of the country where we are—I mean Spain. (130)

To most readers, "the country where we are" could mean only England, and the time could be only the present. Again, this deliberately induced misapprehension is ostentatiously "corrected" by the words "I mean Spain." His reader alerted, Bolingbroke next indicates the rise of Walpole by referring to the astonishing "instances of persons raised to the highest posts of power, authority and command, nay to empire, who had not, either from their obscure birth, or their low talents, or their still lower habits, the least occasion to dream of such elevation. Among other countries, Spain hath had her share of them" (130). The theme that Walpole had got above his station was common in the *Craftsman.* These few examples reveal a satiric technique that exasperated Walpole. Legal proceedings were difficult, as he had found before (and the *Craftsman* attracted no more prosecutions until 1737), so Walpole's journalists intensified their campaign against Bolingbroke.

"Francis Osborne," the pseudonym of James Pitt in the *London Journal*, and "Francis Walsingham," the pseudonym of William Arnall in the *Free Briton*, found themselves in some difficulty when they sought to denounce Bolingbroke's parallels. As Bolingbroke knew, and as the *Craftsman* unhesitatingly replied, if Arnall and Pitt accused him of using any historical circumstance to apply to the present, they implicitly admitted that a parallel existed. Meanwhile, Caleb D'Anvers would solemnly declare the total innocence of all Bolingbroke's writings. This tactic was difficult to counter effectively.

Equally hard to counter was the whole rhetorical technique that served Bolingbroke's satirical intent. The opening letter made important rhetorical advances: Caleb D'Anvers and his correspondents "have drawn their pens in the cause of truth, virtue, and liberty, against . . . assertors of corruption; . . . We may flatter ourselves that these honest endeavors have had some effect; and have reason to hope that far greater will follow from those illustrious examples of repulses, which have been lately given to the grand corrupter, notwithstanding his frequent and insolent declarations that he could seduce whomsoever he had a mind to gain" (23). First, Bolingbroke aligns the *Craftsman* with "the cause of truth, virtue, and liberty." Second, it is clear to every reader who the grand corrupter is (and the "repulses" he has received refer to his defeat over the Excise Bill); but if Arnall or Pitt tried to defend Walpole against false accusation here, they would be acknowledging that the description merits an identification of Walpole. They remained silent. Bolingbroke capitalized on the silence by taking it as an admission of Walpole's guilt. Bolingbroke, yet again, aligns himself with truth against an oppressive and evil enemy.

Reminding his readers that the *Craftsman* is "consecrated to the information of the people of Britain" (28), Bolingbroke says that he, like the other authors, will never speak to the passions without appealing to reason: "I shall therefore execute my design with sincerity and impartiality. I shall certainly not flatter, and I do not mean to offend. Reasonable men and lovers of truth, in whatever party they have been engaged, will not be offended at writings, which claim no regard but on this account, that they are founded in reason and truth, and speak with boldness what reason and truth conspire to dictate" (29). Therefore, the author of the *Dissertation* will be—like Bolingbroke in most of his roles—sincere, reliable, and reasonable.

One of this reasonable narrator's fundamental beliefs is that Whig and Tory have become almost meaningless distinctions, but that the "bulk of both parties are really united; united on principles of liberty, in opposition to an obscure remnant of one party, who disown those principles, and a mercenary detachment from the other, who betray them" (24). Elsewhere (48) Bolingbroke speaks of a division between a court party and a country party: he means by the latter the country as opposed to the city—thus the landed gentlemen—but also the country in the sense of the nation. On this basis, broadening the appeal, he calls on his readers to "maintain and improve the national union, so happily begun, and bless God for disposing the temper of the nation almost universally to it" (27). Party division is really faction, but, he argues, that may be useful for some people. Walpole (he implies) keeps party division alive to serve his own private interests; but although the party rage of the reigns of Charles II and James II can be applied in many respects to Walpole's England, there is a major difference. Whereas liberty was openly attacked after the Restoration, Walpole's methods are more indirect: "The former were the beasts of the field . . . these are the insects of the earth; and like other insects, though sprung from dirt, and the vilest of the animal kind, they can nibble, and gnaw, and poison; and, if they are suffered to multiply and work on, they can lay the most fruitful country waste" (114).

The keystone of Walpole's system is "corrupt, private dependency," (114) and, as we shall see, Bolingbroke was particularly worried that Parliament was becoming dependent on the crown. His ideal was a free constitution consisting of checks and balances, so that king, lords, and commons could control one another's possible excesses. However, should any one part lose its independence, the system can be controlled by the other two. The constitution would be perfect if only Parliament were secure against corruption (147). The first step toward an independent Parliament is to guarantee the freedom of elections. This, the subject of earlier essays, brought the *Dissertation* to a climax at the end of the first sequence of eleven essays.

In Letter 6 Bolingbroke reviews Charles II's reign, in which "all our liberties" were threatened by the crown's influence over elections (60). Despite this influence "the friends of liberty" could still hope for some improvement. But if candidates for Parliament "had been corrupted, and the practice of selling elections had been once established, I imagine that the friends of liberty would have thought the case more desperate" (61). At once, Bolingbroke digresses to the general case to explain that it is better to "struggle even with a great prince who stands on prerogative, than with a weak, but profligate minister, if he hath the means of corruption in his power, and if the luxury and prostitution of the age have enabled him to bring it into fashion" (61). "This," Bolingbroke adds, "was not the case at the time we are speaking of" (61), but it is clearly the case at the time he writes, in 1734.

The *Dissertation* gradually reveals that Walpole and the king work together to undermine liberty. The twin threat is obvious when a dependent parliament under Walpole's management grants the "separate, private revenue, or a civil list, as we commonly call it," to the king. Since 1688

Our kings, instead of contributing most, have contributed nothing to the public charge; and the people of Britain, instead of giving occasionally aids to the crown, have taken upon themselves the whole load of ordinary and extraordinary expenses, for which they annually provide.... Our kings, since the establishment of the civil list, have not only a private and separate estate, but receive a kind of rent-charge out of the public estate, to maintain their honor and dignity, nothing else: and whether the public estate thrive, or not, this rent-charge must be made good to them; at least, as it hath been settled on our present most gracious monarch, ... (157–58)

This reference to the king demanding a rent-charge recalls Bolingbroke's implicit condemnation of George II in Letter 5 of the *Remarks*.[24] This is surely an attempt to provoke a public reaction against excessive taxes, the national debt, the large civil list payment negotiated by Walpole for George in 1727, and against George himself. In the final letter Bolingbroke states explicitly that

the Means of influencing by money, and of governing by corruption, [are] increased now, upon that increase of power which hath accrued to the crown by the new constitution of the revenue since the revolution. Nay farther. Not only the means of corrupting are increased, on the part of the crown, but the facility of employing these means with success is increased, on the part of the people, on the part of the electors, and of the elected. Nay, farther still. These means and this facility are not only increased, but the power of the crown to corrupt, as I have hinted already, and the proneness of the people to be corrupted, must continue to increase on the same principles, unless a stop be put to the growing wealth and power of one, and the growing depravity of the other. (160)

The irony of Bolingbroke's disclaimer would fool no one: "We are, to be sure, in no danger from any advantage his majesty will take of this situation"; nor would his speaking of "the mild and beneficent temper of our heroical monarch" and his flattery of Queen Caroline (160). George's fits of violent temper were well known; Caroline's role as Walpole's main support would hardly endear her to Bolingbroke, and Pope's *Epistle to Augustus* would demonstrate just how "heroical" the Bolingbroke circle considered George. Bolingbroke used the same irony to identify Walpole, too, "our present most incorrupt minister"—italicized in the original for extra, ironic emphasis.

Corruption, and its ultimate threat to liberty, are controlled by the king and his minister. Bolingbroke's hostility to these two is scarcely concealed. Walpole, Bolingbroke has already argued, has great power, but since "Under a prince ... tolerably honest, or tolerably wise, such men as those will have no great sway," George can be neither honest nor wise (89). Tyranny itself is defined as a parliament under the influence of a king—or a minister (94). These two men "poison . . . the morals of mankind" (95).

Bolingbroke's method of satirizing Walpole and George II ranges from the crude joke to a more sophisticated identification of them with the Devil. The minister's nickname, "brass face" (or one of its variants), furnishes opportunities for simple puns (61, 108). More effectively, Bolingbroke describes Walpole's policies as little more than blundering:

> there are some men, such as I shall not mention upon this occasion, (because I reserve them for another and a better) who never deviate into the road of good sense; who, crossed by no difficulties, pressed by no exigencies, meeting scarce opposition enough to excite their industry, and guiding a tame well-tutored flock, that follow their bell-wether obstinately, but never tread on his heels: there are men, I say, whose special privilege it is to proceed with all these advantages, deliberately and superciliously, from blunder to blunder, from year to year, in one perpetual maze of confused, incoherent, inconsistent, unmeaning schemes of business. (50)

But this, Bolingbroke adds disingenuously, has nothing to do with his present subject. Using the rhetorical figure of apophasis, he reminds his readers that he will not mention such men, then does. Not only is Walpole the blunderer, his supporters are contemptuously dismissed as sheep. These people, following one who, like Dryden's MacFlecknoe, never deviates into sense, perpetuate government by confusion, error, and inconsistency. Bolingbroke suggests that the reign of political Dullness is now taking place.

Bolingbroke's supreme insult for his two villains identifies them as the instigators of almost total vice and evil; making it clear that Britain suffers under tyranny, Bolingbroke says "a tyrant, whether prince or minister, resembles the devil in many respects," (63) and more damningly still,

> he imitates the devil, who is so far from promoting the happiness of others, that he makes his own happiness to consist in the misery of others; who governs by no rule but that of his passions, whatever appearances he is forced sometimes to put on, who endeavors to corrupt the innocent and to enslave the free . . . Odious and execrable as this charac-

ter is, it is the character of every prince who makes use of his power to subvert, or even to weaken that constitution, which ought to be the rule of his government. (91)

And, toward the end of the series, "He who undertakes to govern a free people by corruption, and to lead them by a false interest, against their true interest . . . can pretend to no other honor than that of being a humble imitator of the devil" (154). This was Bolingbroke's contribution to the *Craftsman*'s mythology, which showed that in a regime where (in Pope's expression) only "the Fool, the Mad, the Vain, the Evil" prosper materially, true worth is eroded, social order and justice are perverted, and liberty and morality are not merely threatened but are in the hands of men resembling the Devil. With this gloomy outlook Bolingbroke summarizes in the last letter his whole vision of contemporary Britain.

Bolingbroke sees liberty insidiously attacked by men who control money and credit without being held accountable. The chain of evils found in the South Sea Company in his earlier papers is now more explicitly national: "The increase and continuance of taxes" give excessive power to the crown, "But the establishment of public funds, on the credit of these taxes, hath been productive of more and greater mischiefs than the taxes themselves, not only by increasing the means of corruption, and the power of the crown, but by the effect it hath had on the spirit of the nation, on our manners, and our morals" (163). The whole financial revolution that encouraged such a decline now comes under review:

the whole art of stockjobbing, the whole mystery of iniquity . . . arises from this establishment, and is employed about the funds; and, secondly, the main springs that turn, or may turn, the artificial wheel of credit, and make the paper estates that are fastened to it, rise or fall, lurk behind the veil of the treasury. From hence it follows, that if this office should be ever unrighteously administered, if there should ever be at the head of it one of those veteran sharpers, who hath learned by experience how to improve the folly, and aggravate the misfortunes of his fellow subjects, of the innocent, of the poor, of the widow, and of the orphan, to his own, or any other private advantage, it follows, I say, that he must have it in his power, and there can be no doubt of his will, to employ two methods of corruption, without any incumbrance of the civil list. Such a ministerial jobber may employ the opportunities of gaining on the funds, that he can frequently create, by a thousand various artifices . . .

and he may apply the gains, that are thus made, to corruption, in aid of the civil list. (164)

And so it goes: Walpole the political financier controls the entire corrupt operation for the benefit of the king's power, from which Walpole derives his own power. During seven years of the *Craftsman* the hated stockjobber had progressed from the shadowy figure who lurked in Exchange Alley, ruining unwise speculators, to none other than Walpole himself. But now not only unwise speculators are sacrificed: Walpole's victims, in Bolingbroke's rhetorical appeal to compassion, are the most vulnerable members of society: the innocent, the poor, the widow, and the orphan. Not for the first time, he likens Walpole's rise ("by stockjobbing") to that of the "meanest grubs on earth" (165): the image of the insect seems to be the most contemptuous in Bolingbroke's range. But worse, just as such mean creatures can rise to high social status, so too (recalling one effect of South Sea year) "may noblemen and gentlemen debase themselves to their meanness, and acquire the same spirit, by following the same trade" (165). Once this happens, the whole social structure is disrupted and social order destroyed.

It is evident that "the power of money, as the world is now constituted, is real power" (165–66). At the end of the *Dissertation*, Bolingbroke returns to the subject of parties to exhort his reader to resist the faction that arrogates all the money, and therefore all the power, to itself. In a final parallel he says—with more optimism than judgment—that even Walpole must see that he will be removed eventually by a national party. Having diagnosed Britain's ills, Bolingbroke at last reminds his reader who wrote the *Dissertation* and how it should be read:

I have now gone through the task I imposed on myself, and shall only add these few words. There was an engagement taken, in the beginning of these discourses, not to flatter. I have kept this engagement, and have spoken with great freedom; but I hope with the justice and moderation, and decency that I intended, of persons and things. This freedom entitles me to expect that no parallels, no innuendos should be supposed to carry my sense farther than I have expressed it. The reasonable part of mankind will not disappoint so reasonable an expectation. (171)

By this stage every reader is so accustomed to Bolingbroke's irony that he will be able to recognize parallels everywhere. Bolingbroke strongly suggests that the act of recognition is the act of a reasonable man. The devil-like corrupters govern, he said earlier, by passion and not by reason. The *Craftsman*, he said, never appeals to passion without also appealing to reason. Opposition to Walpole's regime is therefore a rational course of action.

Miscellaneous Contributions to the *Craftsman*, 1731–1736

In the period between the completion of *Remarks on the History of England* (May 1731) and the start of *A Dissertation upon Parties* (October 1733), Bolingbroke made nine contributions to the *Craftsman.* The first of these, no. 264 (24 July 1731), is the product of collaboration with Amhurst. Together they review the purpose, progress, and achievement of the *Craftsman* in the light of "Some *late Occurrences* and *Proceedings*" (the arrest of Francklin) and of the "*personal Abuse*, and *extraordinary Appeals to the Secular Arm*" of "our *Adversaries*" (V, 128–29). They conclude (as the *Dissertation* would later) that these "Attacks have really and in Truth been level'd against the *Design* itself, and not, as They pretend, against our *Manner* of conducting it" (V, 128). In self-defense they counter the charges against them: it has become impossible for them "to animadvert on Mismanagements in Government; and yet decline taking any Notice of the *Author* of them," whereas the "*Liberty of Writing*" allowed by "our *Adversaries*" extends only "to Panegyricks and Encomiums on all *ministerial Schemes*" (V, 129–30). Walpole is, after all, styled "the *Prime Minister*" by his apologists and has taken over "*all our Affairs*" both at home and abroad. This essay assembles five "general Principles" expressed by "the *Writers against us*," all intended to indicate an attachment to tyranny and corruption rather than to liberty (V, 130).

It was more than a year before the *Craftsman* published another of Bolingbroke's contributions, a letter in no. 319 (12 August 1732). The letter contains some of his customary rhetorical strategies. In particular, the unnamed author of the letter explains who he is:

I have for several Years past spent most of my Time in the Country, which I had formerly the Honour of representing in Parliament, and did my Duty there to the utmost of my Power; but having had little Money to spare, since the Year 1720, and less Inclination to be led by any Man it hath neither been for my own Interest, nor any Body's else, to be at the Expence of getting into the *House.* Yet, though I trouble my self but little with any Thing, besides my *farming Affairs,* I come up to *London* now and then to see my old Acquaintance, enquire how Matters go, and divert my self with the Amusements of the Town. (V, 137)

This paragraph informs Bolingbroke's reader that the author was a fellow sufferer in the South Sea Bubble, implicit in the reference to 1720, but more significantly that he is an independent country gentleman obviously concerned with politics, though no longer a member of Parliament. Many *Craftsman* essays were addressed to people like this. Yet again, readers could identify with—and therefore trust—such a narrator.

The ostensible subject of the letter is a dispute between Giovanni Buononcini (Handel's most serious rival as a composer of opera) and one of his singers, Aurelio del Po. Purporting to interpret the singer's language in refusing to let his wife, Signora Strada, perform in Buononcini's *Serenata,* this labored paper is an elaborate commentary on the legal interpretation of allegedly libelous innuendo. This subject was close to the hearts of Caleb D'Anvers and his correspondents because Francklin's recent trial had thrust the question of innuendo into the limelight. For example:

Why, did you never hear of Marcus Aurelius, *the famous Statue on Horseback; and what, I pray, is a Man on Horseback; but a* CHEVALIER [a well-known term for the Pretender]*? Now, We all know who the* Chevalier *is,* and—*Ay, 'tis plain (*cry'd a *sober Fellow,* who sate musing all the while in a Corner*) 'tis very plain that* AURELIO *stands for the* PRETENDER, PO *for the* POPE, *and* DEL *for the* DEVIL. (V, 140)

The sort of strained interpretation from which the *Craftsman* is supposed to suffer is ridiculed here.

Bolingbroke's next three contributions, published consecutively in nos. 324 to 326 in September and October 1732, are printed in his *Works* as one essay, "On the Policy of the Athenians." The three essays, says Kramnick, deserve "mention as a tour de force of the Swift-Bolingbroke method of historical satire." They use the same technique as the *Remarks* by using Pericles as an ironic "example" to satirize Walpole.[25]

Early in 1733 Bolingbroke made four contributions to the *Craftsman*'s successful campaign against Walpole's Excise scheme.[26] The

Craftsman argued repeatedly that Walpole's proposal for excise collectors to receive payments at the point of importation would lead to an army of collectors threatening the liberties of all Englishmen. The *Craftsman* also told landholders that the scheme was designed to impoverish them, whereas in fact the opposite was true, just as the "army" of tax collectors was an incredible exaggeration. Caleb D'Anvers took the eventual withdrawal of the Bill as a sign of his personal triumph.

Bolingbroke's essay in no. 353 (7 April 1733) uses a coincidence that suggests a parallel between the structures of theater and government. After the success of Handel's first oratorio, *Esther*, Handel was disappointed by the lukewarm response to *Deborah* on 17 March 1733. The principal cause of failure was his decision to increase the admission prices. On the first night only one hundred and twenty people paid, while hundreds broke into the theater. Handel and Heidegger retorted that the increases were necessary to cover the cost of new lighting in the theater, but the popular assumption was that they wanted larger profits. Walpole had introduced the Excise Bill in the Commons during the same week: Bolingbroke seized the opportunity to draw the parallel between Handel and Walpole, portraying both as greedy men who force unwanted schemes on an unwilling public.

Two more essays on the constitution and government appeared in the late summer of 1733. The first, no. 371 (12 August 1733), praises the Hanover Succession for obtaining the benefit of a constitution founded on liberty, but at once moves to Bolingbroke's by-then-famous ironic method of hypothesizing about some future "evil minister":

> The benefits of this excellent establishment are not so easily discovered, until some abuses happen. But if ever a weak and corrupt administration should arise; if an evil minister should embezzle the public treasure; if he should load the nation, in times of peace, with taxes greater than would be necessary to defray the charge of an expensive war; if the money thus raised should be expended, under the pretence of secret services, to line his own pockets; ... (*Works*, 1:513)

And so it goes on: *if* this, *if* that, *if* all the charges leveled at Walpole over seven years of *Craftsman* papers were found to exist, then the nation would recognize what an excellent constitution it possessed. The irony is apparent in the thundering rhetoric of repetitions.

After the second essay on the constitution (no. 375, 8 September 1733), Bolingbroke published *The Freeholder's Political Catechism*, of which about two thirds appeared in the *Craftsman* no. 377 (22 September 1733). This pamphlet uses the form of dialogue to establish the Englishman's right to liberty, "the natural Right of every human Creature," a liberty based on law (V, 158). The dialogue also restates the desirability of constitutional balance—between king, lords, and commons—as a consequence of which the law binds even the king, "yea, even the *supreme*, or *legislative Power* is bound, by the Rules of Equity, to govern by *Laws* enacted, and published in due Form; for what is not *legal* is *arbitrary*" (V, 160). If ever anything guaranteed horror in the mind of the neutral eighteenth-century gentleman, it was mention of arbitrary power.

Five weeks later in the *Craftsman*, the *Dissertation* began to discuss these same subjects: liberty, the constitution, and the power of the crown. While the *Dissertation* was being serialized, Bolingbroke wrote two more essays for the *Craftsman*. One (no. 406, 13 April 1734) uses Cicero's anecdote about Philip of Macedon to condemn bribery and corruption, showing that it is both bad politics and entirely immoral for a king to bribe—or attempt to bribe—his own subjects. The other (no. 430, 28 September 1734) discusses the people's ancient right to liberty, repeating the method of the *Remarks*.

Most of Bolingbroke's writing in 1734 was, as we have seen, concerned with liberty and the constitution. The earlier essays in this period were part of the opposition's campaign to repeal the Septennial Act and replace it by a return to parliaments elected every three years instead of seven. (To many independents, as to Pulteney himself, frequent elections meant less corruption.) The later essays were occasioned by the desire to urge voters to elect men of integrity in the general election, late in 1734. It was during a debate on Wyndham's proposal to repeal the Septennial Act that Walpole delivered his famous speech which, it is normally thought, did much to persuade both "the anti-minister" and the opposition that Bolingbroke was, politically, finished.[27]

In 1735, discouraged and discarded, Bolingbroke wrote nothing for his *Craftsman*. Once settled in France, he put together his last four essays in the spring of 1736. These long essays castigate Walpole for settling for a peace less advantageous than that of Utrecht (the treaty that Walpole chose to criticize adversely and of which Bolingbroke was so proud). Since Britain allows France to occupy Lorraine, Bolingbroke argues, French possessions will reach as far as the Rhine and therefore pose a threat to the Netherlands and Germany. His method of tracing a rise in French power to a series of diplomatic weaknesses among the Protestant allies is repeated in the *Letters on the Study and Use of History* in his sketch of a diplomatic history of Europe from 1659 to 1713.

End of an Era

The *Remarks*, which dominated the *Craftsman* during 1730 and 1731, describes a sequence of evil ministers whom Walpole is supposed to resemble; the *Dissertation*, the dominant series in 1733 and 1734, concentrates on the constitution. Both sets of essays are mainly concerned with the concept of liberty. In the miscellaneous essays liberty is again predominant, but the subjects are more varied. During his nine years on the *Craftsman* Bolingbroke sustained a tone of irony and innuendo (occasionally accompanied by less oblique hostility), stuck to his rhetorical method of creating a persuasive and reliable narrator, and employed clear, plain arguments. In 1727 his early contributions to the *Craftsman*—and his three *Occasional Writer* papers—had sought to satirize Walpole. By 1735 Walpole and King George were Bolingbroke's twin targets. The campaign in the *Craftsman*, which brought Bolingbroke's opposition increasingly into the open, exemplifies the rhetorician's art of persuasion.

In many of his essays Bolingbroke enmeshes Britain's foreign affairs (and the need to give them plenty of attention) with domestic matters, and past history with present politics. He envisages a return to rightful power distributed among honorable men acting out of altruism and independent will. By supporting the traditional strength of a trading nation and securing the independence of Parliament against a corrupt minister and a no-less-corrupt-and-power-seeking king, such independent men will put Britain where Bolingbroke thinks she belongs, in a position of prosperity from which she can command the respect—even the obedience—of Europe, maintain political balance, and safeguard the cherished liberty of the individual. It is the vision of a man convinced that liberty is threatened and has already been partly curtailed by a system that encourages men to look only for short-term personal profit. What Bolingbroke has in mind, in these *Craftsman* essays, is nothing less than national renovation.

No series of essays, nor any single author, would dominate the *Craftsman* again. In 1737 the printer published seven more volumes of the paper's articles, finishing appropriately with Bolingbroke's last essay.

Chapter Five

History and Patriotism

In November 1735, just under a year after completing the *Dissertation upon Parties*, Bolingbroke finished *Letters on the Study and Use of History*. This work was first printed privately in "some Very Few Copy's" by Pope at Bolingbroke's direction in 1738,[1] but when it was published in 1752 it quickly became controversial.[2] Kramnick's introduction to these *Letters* claims that "Bolingbroke's historical writings are perhaps the best example of the historical skepticism which ushered in the French Enlightenment."[3] The *Letters*, well received in France, reveal a French influence, and in this work, as Kramnick says, Bolingbroke unites the seemingly irreconcilable historical positions of the humanist and the skeptic. Bolingbroke the humanist emphasizes the value of history as example, while Bolingbroke the skeptic casts doubt, as the French Enlightenment tended to do, on the validity and value of history.[4]

Bolingbroke had been speculating about the nature and value of history as early as 1719: "The little I read in my youth of ancient history," he told Alary, "has made me think that it is impossible to have the least knowledge of the events of those times; that the systems, either historical or chronological, which scholars confidently parade before us are based only on continual question-begging"; and he added that he was contemplating writing a work in some form that would contain "all these ideas and proofs to support them."[5] In 1722 Bolingbroke was questioning the validity of the chronology of ancient history, which becomes prominent in the letters on history.[6]

The book contains eight letters. The first is dated from "Chantelou, November 6, 1735," and addressed to "a young nobleman," in reality Lord Cornbury, who had asked Bolingbroke "to direct me in the Study of History."[7] The first five letters discuss the value of history as a subject of study, and the other three contain an outline of a diplomatic history of Europe from about 1500 to 1713, with most attention focused on the period after 1659. In David Mallet's editions of the *Letters on History* (1752) and Bolingbroke's *Works* (1754) all eight are followed by "A Plan for a General History of Europe," which is in fact the text of a letter from Bolingbroke to Pope of 18 August 1724,[8] and by another letter "Of the True Use of Retirement and Study" addressed to Lord Bathurst.[9]

The main issues raised in the eight letters on history are the inaccuracy of ancient history, the value of history as a collection of moral teachings that encourage public and private virtue, and the dictum that history is philosophy teaching by examples. Bolingbroke considers the study of history an essential part of the training for a "public" man, a man of action—that is, a statesman. This belief leads Bolingbroke to a casual dismissal as worthless of almost all pre-Renaissance history, whose influence on the history of his own time he considers minimal and oblique.

Recent commentators have indicated the features of Bolingbroke's humanism and skepticism, and they have properly discussed his historical writing as philosophy of history.[10] I shall here give weight to the role of rhetoric in the historical writings, where Bolingbroke's immediate concerns arise from his conception of morality and corruption, and I shall examine the relation between these writings and his immediate political concerns. The *Letters* are not normally thought to be political satire, but John Leland, the most formidable of Bolingbroke's early critics, saw that "There are several parts of his letters . . . in which [Bolingbroke] expresseth himself with all the rage of a passionate party-writer."[11] Rhetoric was the vehicle of his overtly political writing; now, in 1735, unhappily out of politics again, he took rhetoric into the domain of historical philosophy.

The Study of History

The very brief opening letter places the author in a position from which he dismisses contemptuously the efforts of antiquarians, grammarians, and academics. The satirist's aggression had certainly not deserted Bolingbroke when he said of the "Men of the first rank in learning" that "A man must be as indifferent as I am to common censure or approbation, to avow a thorough contempt for the whole business of these learned lives" (174). These men's systems of chronology and history are held to be wild and impossible, like "so many enchanted castles; they appear to be something, they are nothing but appearances: like them too, dissolve the charm, and they vanish from the sight" (175). So much for the false foundation of "disjointed passages" joined together, the "broken traditions of uncertain originals"

(175), and, in short, all "the learned lumber" (176). It is clear that "The humanist historical tradition saw the pursuit of historical fact as an objective always secondary to the primary one of drawing lessons from the past,"[12] but it is also obvious that Bolingbroke, with a rhetorician's tactic (if not a rhetorician's tact), considers himself superior to the fact gatherers, whom he sweeps aside.

Letter 2 contains the first main point. Bolingbroke makes one statement that recalls his discussion of self-love in *Reflections concerning Innate Moral Principles* and raises the subject of past and future fame: "The love of history seems inseparable from human nature, because it seems inseparable from self-love.... We imagine that the things, which affect us, must affect posterity: this sentiment runs through mankind" at all levels; men like to preserve "the memory of our own adventures, of those of our own time, and of those that preceded it" (176). And because we all like to know "what has happened to other men" as well as to ourselves, we "indulge our own curiosity" (176) but to study history only to satisfy curiosity would be idle: Bolingbroke asserts that "The true and proper object of this application [of the mind] is a constant improvement in private and in public virtue," and "the study of history seems to me, of all other, the most proper to train us up to private and public virtue" (177). His explanation of how history makes men both better and wiser is simple: citing a famous and much quoted phrase from Dionysus of Halicarnassus, Bolingbroke says "history is philosophy teaching by examples" (177).

One of the examples Bolingbroke lists is the Roman habit of placing statues of heroes "in the vestibules of their houses"; through these statues "The virtue of one generation was transferred, by the magic of example, into several: and a spirit of heroism was maintained through many ages of that commonwealth" (179). If that example seems hard to treat seriously, Bolingbroke does add the weightier point that study can be a valuable addition to experience, since to understand the past helps to prepare us for the future. Simultaneously, one important duty of history, "according to Tacitus and according to truth ... is to erect a tribunal," passing judgment even on the dead, "to render these examples of general instruction to mankind" (185). A central idea of Tacitus, borrowed by Rapin and again now by Bolingbroke, is that history rewards virtuous people by perpetuating the memory of their noble actions, and punishes vicious people by perpetuating the memory of their ignoble actions. Thus history is a kind of moral policeman, and the historian is tacitly invested with an important duty to preserve morality and truth (191).

In this context Bolingbroke turns to recent history in order to gain "a complete example, and to develope [*sic*] all the wise, honest, and salutary precepts" of the 1688 revolution, but first it is necessary to go back to the history of the earlier seventeenth century. Here Bolingbroke cites an example of how history "enables us to guess at future events" (189), for after 1688 care of the national finances came under the control of "a moneyed interest, in opposition to the landed interest or as a balance to it" (188). These moneyed men began the financial revolution by which they were able to amass "immense estates by the management of funds, by trafficking in paper, and by all the arts of jobbing" (188). To Bolingbroke, as readers of the *Craftsman* knew already, the new financial order was a "scheme of iniquity" (188). Worse was to follow, since "we who came after them, and have long tasted the bitter fruits of the corruption they planted, were far from taking such an alarm at our distress and our danger, as they deserved; till the most remote and fatal effects of causes, laid by the last generation, was [*sic*] very near becoming an object of experience in this" (188). The proper study of history "would have pointed out national corruption, as the natural and necessary consequence of investing the crown with the management of so great a revenue; but also the loss of liberty, as the natural and necessary consequence of national corruption" (188–89). Bolingbroke's point here belongs to historical philosophy but this example comes straight from his political ideology: he uses history as a political weapon against the architects of the financial system he distrusts. Although not representative of the *Letters* as a whole, this passage is central to all Bolingbroke's conceptions of history and politics.

The Validity of History

In Letter 3, casting himself in his favorite role of educator, Bolingbroke explains how history furnishes many particular examples, from which men must construct general propositions:

> There are certain general principles, and rules of life and conduct, which always must be true, because they are conformable to the invariable nature of things. He who studies history as he would study philosophy, will soon distinguish and collect them, and by doing so will soon form to

himself a general system of ethics and politics on the surest foundations, on the trial of these principles and rules in all ages, and on the confirmation of them by universal experience. (193)

Ultimately, he says (following Locke's still widely accepted principle), the study of history is valuable as a mental discipline; without slavishly copying anything, we learn how to think and judge, for "by knowing the things that have been we become better able to judge of the things that are" (194). This sensible observation leads Bolingbroke to denounce what he sees as absurd systems of chronology and history. The first of these are found in ancient "profane" history (197). Inevitably, he says, early Greek historians wrote nothing accurate or authentic; their history is all too vague, too full of invention (198), too full of a desire to please their audiences at the expense of accuracy (199). Even Diodorus Siculus, writing in the first century B.C., complained about the poor Greek histories available to him (199).

So, asks Bolingbroke, where do we turn for reliable ancient history? The usual answer is to the Bible. Bolingbroke's treatment of this subject brought upon his work the wrath of a dozen commentators, mostly learned men of the church, who objected to his language, which "was not the kind to endear him to his pious readers."[13] He dared to say that "these divine books must be reputed insufficient . . . by every candid and impartial man who considers either their authority as histories, or the matter they contain" (200). Like the Greeks, the Church fathers and the authors of the Old Testament fail to provide "authentic, clear, distinct and full accounts of the originals of ancient nations" or of events (211). The principal points of Bolingbroke's skeptical attack are that ancient history, particularly biblical, is unhelpfully selective (he cites twenty centuries of history crammed into "eleven short chapters of Genesis" [208]), and that the oral method of transmission is untrustworthy. He remarks acidly:

Thus . . . when we consider these books barely as histories, delivered to us on the faith of a superstitious people, among whom the custom and art of pious lying prevailed remarkably, we may be allowed to doubt whether greater credit is to be given to what they tell us concerning the original, compiled in their own country and as it were out of sight of the rest of the world; than we know, with such a certainty as no scholar presumes to deny, that we ought to give to what they tell us concerning the copy? (201)

The third letter shows that the earliest histories are not reliable and therefore do not help us to develop our judgments. One of the more perceptive critics among Bolingbroke's contemporaries, Bishop Clayton thought that Bolingbroke examined "ancient Histories" only to attack the Scriptures.[14] Also noticing that Bolingbroke's purpose in reading the Bible was "only to collect from thence a political History for the Instruction of Statesmen, with Regard to the Treaty of *Utrecht*,"[15] Clayton recognized that Bolingbroke's purpose was both polemical and political.

Bolingbroke appeals to "every candid and impartial man," as opposed to the readers of the earliest histories, "a superstitious people" given to "pious lying." The rhetorical posture, which combines an appeal to reason with the dismissal (in Letter 1) of most ancient history, creates a narrator who presents himself as a superior example of a "candid and impartial man."

In the scheme of the whole work on history, this section of the *Letters* has a valid place: Bolingbroke is trying to establish the limits of knowledge, "the bounds beyond which there was neither history nor chronology" (196). To this end he tries to distinguish "between the legal, doctrinal, or prophetical parts of the Bible, and the historical" (203), and tries to establish reason as the only genuinely trustworthy guide. Letter 4 continues from this point. Unless the reader knows that a work of history is authoritative, he should not believe what he reads: otherwise he risks delusion (211). Not only has history been deliberately falsified (213) but the church itself has often been responsible for falsification, employing "pious frauds . . . to maintain a reverence and zeal for their religion in the minds of men" (214). Worse still, "This lying spirit has gone forth from ecclesiastical to other historians . . . and history becomes very often a lying panegyric of a lying satire" (214). Much history, evidently inspired by partisan "passions" (217), is transparently false as soon as we find any other history of the same period. Ultimately "the favorable opportunities of corrupting history have been often interrupted, and are now over in so many countries, that truth penetrates even into those where lying continues still to be part of the policy ecclesiastical and civil" (218). The reader's critical judgment, then, must separate "the ore from the dross" and find a middle way (217).

In order to teach us adequately, "History must have a certain degree of probability and authenticity, or the examples we find in it would not carry a force sufficient to make due impressions on our minds, nor to illustrate nor to strengthen the precepts of philosophy and the rules of good policy" (219). Whatever else may be said of histories, they must be read with "discernment and choice" (220). That Bolingbroke, advising his reader, has done so himself emerges from his method of establishing his conclusion that so much history "is come to us so imperfect and so corrupt" (216). To reach this statement he guides his reader through a series of assertions about illiberal regimes and their efforts at censorship. Bolingbroke introduces these by saying that "He who reflects on the circumstances . . . he who carries these reflections on . . . he who considers all these things, I say, will not be at a loss to find the reasons why history" is so inadequate (216). The author seems to address a reader who has *not* reflected and *not* considered the examples; and, implicitly instructed to think, no such ignorant reader would admit folly by rejecting the conclusion that most history is imperfect. In this way Bolingbroke manipulates his reader into agreement with this polemical point.

Bolingbroke carefully guides his reader through his apparently philosophical arguments, establishing himself as a man of judgment who can see through the falsities of ancient history. The knowledgeable instructor—a role accentuated by the epistolary form of the work—Bolingbroke contrasts himself with an acquaintance who read without discernment and choice (219–20) and whose mind was therefore a mass of confusion.

Bolingbroke emerges as the only man who can tell his reader what is reliable and what is not: in his own hands history will be neither a lying panegyric nor a lying satire. Thinking the first five letters of little or no relevance to the others, G.M. Trevelyan edited only the last three, but those earlier letters are relevant: they prepare the reader for the "truthful" panegyric and the "truthful" satire that fill the later three.[16] For a decade Bolingbroke had been attacking corruption. Here, in the *Letters*, he tried a different approach by advocating study as a means to acquire and understand virtue. In Letter 5 he suggests this by an implicit parallel between Tacitus ("a favorite author" [227]) and himself: "When Tacitus wrote, even the appearances of virtue had been long proscribed, and taste was grown corrupt as well as manners. Yet history preserved her integrity and her lustre" (226). If "Tacitus" were changed to "Bolingbroke" this statement would apply to contemporary Britain.

Bolingbroke uses a similar parallel when he discusses Livy's history of Rome:

> I should be glad to exchange, if it were possible, what we have of this history for what we have not. Would not you be glad, my lord, to see, in one stupendous draught, the whole progress of that government from liberty to servitude? the whole series of causes and effects, apparent and real, public and private? those which all men saw, and all good men lamented and opposed at the time; and those which were so disguised to the prejudices, to the partialities of a divided people, and even to the corruption of mankind, that many did not, and that many could pretend they did not, discern them, till it was too late to resist them? I am sorry to say it, this part of the Roman story would be not only more curious and more authentic than the former, but of more immediate and more important application to the present state of Britain. (228)

Just why such a history would have been more authentic is not clear, but Bolingbroke evidently believes that the history of a declining nation would somehow represent the truth and therefore be admirable. Bolingbroke implies that Britain itself is corrupt and close to servitude. His next remark parallels himself with the Livy he cannot read but whom he aligns with truth, since "a history must be written on this plan, and must aim at least at these perfections, or it will not answer sufficiently the intentions of history" (228).

One of the "intentions of history" is to provide the "examples" that "prepare men for the discharge of that duty which they owe to their country" (235). Bolingbroke's defense of this point (against "ridicule cast on private men who make history a political study") suggests that undemocratic governments cause individuals to serve not their country but the court, or, ultimately, only the king. The example of Turkey—the worst such government—is of outright tyranny. France is a little better: "Arts and Sciences are encouraged, and here and there an example may be found of a man who has risen by some extraordinary talents, amidst innumerable examples of men who have arrived at the greatest honors and highest posts by no other merit than that of assiduous fawning, attendance, or of skill in some despicable puerile amusement" (235–36). One implication is that Britain, too, is as bad as this. Bolingbroke had said in the *Craftsman* (no. 114) that arts and sciences in Britain in 1728 were actively discouraged, and one of his repeated complaints was that men who rose to positions of power in the Walpole regime (including Walpole himself) did so without genuine merit. Bolingbroke argues that to study the history or politics of such regimes as the absolute monarchy of China prepares a man of action to serve the British public because he will recognize a parallel to the Chinese in the tyranny of Walpole's corrupt administration. Here Bolingbroke releases the first hint of his idea of a patriot king, who in Britain "is but the first servant of the people" (237). Because men serve not the king but the state, under a free government "it is incumbent on every man to instruct himself, as well as the means and opportunities he has permit, concerning the nature and interests of the government, and those rights and duties that belong to him, or to his superiors, or to his inferiors" (237). Bolingbroke ironically implies that the present king is not the first servant of the people, that Britain does not have a free government, and that political rights are eroded and duties neglected in favor of the pursuit of private interest. The chief emphasis of Letter 5 is not on a philosophical theory of how history should be read, but on a rhetorical exhortation to "dutiful" conduct to repair contemporary Britain.

Bolingbroke's History

Bolingbroke recognized that examples from ancient history could not be applied with precision to modern times. Instead, a particular example engendered a general principle of moral conduct. This difference may account for many of Bolingbroke's inexact parallels. Examples from recent history are more likely to be applicable, but still their function is to suggest general principles. In Letter 6 Bolingbroke sets out "from what period modern history is peculiarly useful to the service of our country" (238). He thinks history before 1500 can little reward detailed study (239); but about 1500 "all those events happened, and all those revolutions began, that have produced so vast a change in the manners, customs, and interests of particular nations, and in the whole policy, ecclesiastical and civil, of these parts of the world" (239). J. G. A. Pocock finds Bolingbroke's attitude "deplorable . . . and there is something peculiarly unpleasing about the spectacle of Bolingbroke blotting out vast tracts of human experience as unworthy of serious attention."[17] Although one must agree with Pocock, Bolingbroke's approach involves a serious polemical purpose that would receive no support from any investigation of earlier history.

The perfunctory survey in Letter 6 of ecclesiastical government since the early sixteenth century shows the decline of the Pope's power since the Reformation. "The spirit and pretensions of his court are the same, but not the power. [The Pope] governs by expedient and management more, and by authority less" (242). This example prefigures an equally perfunctory survey of civil government in France and England. The constitution has changed so much in France since 1500 that to study the earlier period is pointless (244), and the history of England is worth studying only from the time of "the great change" under Henry VIII (245). His final example in this letter is Spain and the Holy Roman Empire, or in effect the rest of western Europe. These surveys reveal Bolingbroke's interest in constitutional changes; in all of them, the birth of modern forms of government and the distribution of power are his criteria for deciding that the study of history is of practical benefit.

Letter 7 contains a sketch of European history from the Pyrenean Treaty of 1659 to the revolution of 1688 in Britain. The first half of this letter describes the rise of France. Among the advantages Louis XIV enjoyed after 1660 was the absence of any effective opponent in Europe, but the real origin of his many advantages over his rivals lay "in the conduct of Richelieu and Mazarin" (254), whose political skill Bolingbroke admired. Yet he thought Richelieu and Mazarin disastrously influential in creating "a great change of the balance of power in Europe, and . . . the prospect of one much greater and more fatal" (256). The two French statesmen were responsible for the Pyrenean Treaty by which Spain and France were brought together in "a peace . . . that has disturbed the peace of the world almost fourscore years, and the consequences of which have well nigh beggared in our times the nation [Cromwell] enslaved in his" (257). Richelieu "varnished ambition with the most plausible and popular pretences" (255), and Mazarin "finished the work that Richelieu began" (259). After these two, Colbert "must be mentioned particularly . . . because it was he who improved the wealth and consequently the power of France extremely, by the order he put into the finances, and by the encouragement he gave to trade and manufactures" (259). Colbert maintained France's power by strengthening the union with Spain and weakening both Britain and the Netherlands. The Dutch, led by de Witt, had (in the 1660s) no love for England, and this played into the hands of the French (260–61). After showing the dangers of disunion and distrust among the European powers, Bolingbroke devotes the rest of this penultimate letter to their military and diplomatic activities resulting in France's almost undiminished power at at the end of the seventeenth century.

Although this letter does not contain the same brand of partisan history as Bolingbroke's *Craftsman* history, it is not without partisan rhetoric. The modern period "begins by a great change of the balance of power in Europe, and by the prospect of one much greater and more fatal" (256). Bolingbroke is referring to the potential union of Spain and France, but how could this be "more fatal" unless he is thinking of the consequences for Britain and Europe in 1736? Further, Colbert's work of enriching France meant that "Her baubles, her modes, the follies and extravagances of her luxury, cost England . . . little less than eight hundred thousand pounds sterling a year, and other nations in their proportions" (259). If history furnishes examples, this is surely an instance of England's gullibility under Walpole's weak foreign policy, which makes Britain the dupe of Europe.

A similar example is found in Bolingbroke's discussion of the Dutch role in this period. Holland did not pursue her "true interest," union with England: "John de Wit, at the head of the Louvestein faction, governed. The interest of his party was to keep the house of Orange down: he courted therefore the friendship of France, and neglected that of England" (260). And, Bolingbroke adds, "As the private interests of the two De Wits hindered that commonwealth from being on her guard, as early as she ought to have been, against France, so the mistaken policy of the court of England, and the short views, and the profuse temper of the prince who governed, gave great advantages to Louis the Fourteenth in the pursuit of his designs" (261). Bolingbroke had written of de Witt before, in the *Craftsman* (no. 142), where his intention was clearly to parallel Johan de Witt and Robert Walpole, and to show the effect of the pursuit of private interest: one's country is seriously disadvantaged. The example applies again, albeit with reduced emphasis, in this letter. This survey of French and Dutch diplomacy in the later seventeenth century is an extended example, designed to reveal a general parallel between the weak condition of England from 1659 to 1688 and the condition of England under Walpole. Bolingbroke expects his reader to recognize that the French are ambitious and the Dutch selfishly avaricious. More instances of this "exemplar" strategy lead him to the last and longest of his letters, in which he elaborately defends the events leading to and the negotiations for the Treaty of Utrecht of 1713.

John Leland was quick to condemn the eighth letter as a party pamphlet,[18] and Caleb Fleming called it "a piece of self-defence, wherein [Bolingbroke] is so far from admitting the general, the public accusation of *crime*, that he would avail himself of *merit*."[19] There is some truth in both these observations. The eighth letter does make use of Bolingbroke's rhetoric of self-presentation. First, he needs to establish his narrative basis by indicating the broad outlines of Britain's relations with France during the last two decades of the seventeenth century. One significant event was the national clamor against James II's stooping to be France's pensioner. By contrast, under William III "the nation engaged with all imaginable zeal in the common cause of Europe, to reduce the exorbitant power of France, to prevent and to revenge her past attempts" (277); but the zeal was badly directed. Bolingbroke attributes to the British under William a spirit of liberty, like that spirit his *Remarks* had repeatedly emphasized and tried to revive. He puts in the customary bad word for James and stresses the dangers embodied by Britain's old enemy, France. His is a straightforward appeal to a long-established political enmity.

Bolingbroke continues with an account of Britain's lamentable failure to achieve anything of any consequence during the war against France in the 1690s, and at once he resumes his favorite subject:

> They who got by the war, and made immense fortunes by the necessities of the public, were not so numerous nor so powerful, as they have been since. The moneyed interest was not yet a rival able to cope with the landed interest, either in the nation or in parliament. The great corporations that had been erected more to serve the turn of party, than for any real national use, aimed indeed even then at the strength and influence which they have since acquired in the legislature; but they had not made the same progress by promoting national corruption, as they and the court have made since. (281–82)

Bolingbroke never doubts that his view of history is appropriate, as he uses this recent history to teach moral—and practical—lessons of politics. His purpose is not to write the history of Britain's failure to curb France, it is to identify the conditions in which corruption—the problem of the 1730s—may flourish. But Bolingbroke cannot resist introducing his own role, confessing what he would have done had he sat in Parliament then:

> I should have voted for disbanding the army then, as I voted in the following parliament for censuring the partition treaties. I am forced to own this, because I remember how imperfect my notions were of the situation of Europe in that extraordinary crisis, and how much I saw the true interest of my own country in a half-light. But, my lord, I own it with some shame; because in truth nothing could be more absurd than the conduct we held. (282)

Once more Bolingbroke justifies himself, presenting an honest, moderate persona, willing to admit to imperfect judgment. By drawing attention to his role as narrator, Bolingbroke prepares his reader for the most polemical part of the narrative, which describes the period of his deepest personal involvement in diplomatic affairs. After a long, and somewhat dull, narrative, Bolingbroke starts to reach some conclusions about the period up to 1706, when France began to think peace might be preferable to war.

The Whigs, he suggests, could have made a reasonable peace in 1706 had they wanted one, but private interest affected their judgment. Bolingbroke confidently tells his reader why Britain accepted an obviously undesirable political position: "the prejudices and rashness of party," the flush of military success, "ancient and fresh resentments" based on forty years of Louis XIV's reign in France, and "a notion, groundless but prevalent, that [Louis] was and would be master as long as his grandson [i.e., Philip] was king of Spain, and that there could be no effectual measure taken, though the grand alliance supposed that there might, to prevent a future union of the two monarchies, as long as a prince of the house of Bourbon sat on the Spanish throne" (299). This last reason, he says, is not surprising when one realizes "how ill the generality of mankind are informed, how incapable they are of judging, and yet how ready to pronounce judgment; in fine, how inconsiderately they follow one another in any popular opinion which the heads of party broach, or to which the first appearances of things have given occasion" (299). So, at last, Bolingbroke reveals explicitly the need for his long narrative of events: if his purpose is apparently to encourage Lord Cornbury—or any other reader—to understand man ("the subject of history," 229) or to extract exemplary philosophy from such history as this, Bolingbroke has a prejudiced view of history indeed, for the man we learn about is, indirectly, Bolingbroke himself. He blames party for the difficulties he himself faced as Secretary of State, and he "blames" forty years of the French king's conduct for Britain's decision. The principal observation is one that Bolingbroke must have felt deeply:

> To have humbled and reduced, in five campaigns, a power that had disturbed and insulted Europe almost forty years; to have restored, in so short a time, the balance of power in Europe to a sufficient point of equality, after it had been more than fifty years . . . in a gradual deviation from this point; in short to have retrieved, in [1706], a game that was become desperate at the beginning of the century. To have done all this, before the war had exhausted our strength, was the utmost sure that any man could desire who intended the public good alone: and no honest reason ever was, nor ever will be given, why the war was protracted any longer; why we neither made peace after a short, vigorous, and successful war, nor put it entirely out of the power of France to continue at any rate a long one. (303)

Aside from the purely political advantages listed here, one familiar phrase is "any man . . . who intended the public good." This mysterious patriot who figures prominently in Bolingbroke's obviously polemical writing is presented as the one man who stands above petty squabbles or private interest, the true patriot who would not pursue the war and who saw the truth then and sees it now. The patriot is, of course, Bolingbroke himself or, on a wider rhetorical plane, any reader who sees the logic of the whole commonsensical argument.

As the narrator approaches 1710, he assumes that his reader will agree "that the war could [not] be supported in Spain with any prospect of advantage on our side" (306) because "the falsehood of all those lures, by which we had been enticed to make war in Spain, had appeared sufficiently in [1706]; but was grossly evident in [1710]" (306). As he discusses Britain's failure to bring about peace in 1706 and 1710 Bolingbroke approaches the stance of *The Conduct of the Allies*: "they, who clamored rather than argued for the continuation of [the war], contented themselves to affirm, that France was not enough reduced, and that no peace ought to be made as long as a prince of the house of Bourbon remained on a Spanish throne" (311–12). Bolingbroke's summary of British attitudes at the end of the first decade of the eighteenth century casually develops into an indictment of the Whigs. He first contrasts the old Whigs of Charles II's reign with those "who succeeded to the name rather than the principles of party" (312). These later Whigs "have run into an extreme as vicious and as contrary to all the rules of good policy, as that which their predecessors exclaimed against. The old whigs complained of the inglorious figure we made, ... The modern whigs boasted, and still boast, of the glorious figure we made, whilst we reduced ourselves, by their councils, and under their administrations, to be the bubbles of our pensioners, that is, of our allies" (313).

This behavior has led to a catastrophe. Trade has declined, while short-sighted and self-interested Whig politicians have done little or nothing to maintain Britain's position as a major European trading nation. The whole trouble is that

taxes upon taxes, and debts upon debts, have been perpetually accumulated, till a small number of families have grown into immense wealth, and national beggary has been brought upon us; ... the reign of false and squandering policy has lasted long, it lasts still, and will finally complete our ruin. Beggary has been the consequence of slavery in some countries: slavery will be probably the consequence of beggary in ours; and if it is so, we know at whose door to lay it. (313–14)

This picture is familiar to Bolingbroke's readers: it is the old story of private interest causing public ruin. If the reader is persuaded thus far to accept Bolingbroke's point of view, his sympathy for the author will probably follow automatically, for Bolingbroke says confidently, "Upon this view your lordship will be persuaded ..." (314). Bolingbroke exploits that sympathy by dissociating himself—as we expect—from adverse criticism aimed at the Whigs, who initiated the decline of Britain: "If we had finished the war in [1706], we should have reconciled, like a wise people, our foreign and our domestic interests as nearly as possible" (314). The Whigs, of course, did not finish the war, and were therefore not wise. By implication, Bolingbroke *is* wise, but he adds an explicitly personal statement that strengthens his reliability as narrator:

The persons ... who came into power in [1710] hearkened, and they did well to hearken, to the first overtures that were made them. The disposition of their enemies invited them to do so, but that of their friends, and that of a party at home who had nursed, and been nursed by the war, might have deterred them from it; for the difficulties and dangers to which they must be exposed in carrying forward this great work, could escape none of them. In a letter to a friend it may be allowed me to say, that they did not escape me: and that I foresaw, as contingent but not improbable events, a good part of what has happened to me since. (314)

Bolingbroke stresses further his certainty that he was right. This sounds little like exemplary history from which a reader acquires moral virtue: it is, rather, Bolingbroke defending himself in an apparently private letter on a public subject. His strategy here is the familiar one of creating an image of himself as honest and principled, to ensure that the reader accepts the serious argument that the present corrupted, declining state of the nation is a direct result of the rise of the moneyed interest. Bolingbroke's rhetorical stance gives this argument its full force. He is careful not to overestimate the value of the Treaty of Utrecht: instead, he says (accurately) "we ought to have reaped more advantage from it than we did" (315) and he therefore tends to sound like the sincere commentator, the moderate who avoids those extremes he censures. As Leland remarked in 1753: "His lordship, indeed, has found an excellent way for throwing the blame of making such an insufficient peace, not upon those that concluded it, but upon those that opposed it."[20] Further, Bolingbroke revives the argument that, because opposition to the peace meant opposition to the measures of the queen's ministry, opposition was therefore close to treason. Thus, he aligns himself again with the cause of right.

The study of history, Bolingbroke concludes, is valuable as long as "we accustom ourselves to compare the conduct of different governments, and different parties, in the same conjunctures," and to compare what did happen with what might have happened. This, he says, should excuse the length of his letter—but in case it does not, "I have one more [reason] that may. A rage of warring possessed a party in our nation till the death of the late queen: a rage of negotiating has possessed the same party of men, ever since. You have seen the consequences of one: you see actually those of the other. The rage of warring confirmed the beggary of our nation, which began as early as the revolution" (330–31). His glance back in time shows that since Utrecht, 1713, "our ministers have been in one perpetual maze" (331). The reason for this bewilderment is probably not the Utrecht settlement but Bolingbroke's absence from government.

Finally, in two fast-moving concluding paragraphs, Bolingbroke traces the rise of luxury, foppishness, and debauchery during the Restoration period, intimating that they have become subsequently exaggerated. Indeed they have, since in Britain in the 1730s

> the state is become, under ancient and known forms, a new and undefinable monster; composed of a king without monarchical splendor, a senate of nobles without aristocratical independency, and a senate of commons without democratical freedom. In the mean time, my lord, the very idea of wit, and all that can be called taste, has been lost among the great; arts and sciences are scarce alive; luxury has been increased but not refined; corruption has been established, and is avowed. When governments are worn out, thus it is: the decay appears in every instance. Public and private spirit, science and wit, decline all together. (333)

Repeating here the vision expressed in the previous decade in the *Craftsman*, Bolingbroke suggests that it is now the duty of a new generation of young patriots to restore Britain.

The *Letters* do not attempt to solve the problems of the present, although Bolingbroke's philosophy suggests that history can help to solve them. This work uses history to highlight the political and constitutional decline into which Bolingbroke thinks Britain has sunk. Considered as pure historical philosophy, the *Letters* surely justify Pocock's criticism of them. Bolingbroke's partisan history, expressed repetitively and at unnecessary length, pictures the only period he is genuinely interested in: his own. Much of the art of the satirist—the rhetorical style and method he had employed in the *Craftsman*—recurs here. Although the difference in tone and approach between the *Letters* and the *Dissertation upon Parties* is marked, Bolingbroke did not, in 1735, suddenly abandon political writing for philosophy. In the *Letters* he casts himself again in the role of educator, a knowledgeable, reliable narrator, instructing the next generation of patriots in the art of opposition.

On the Spirit of Patriotism

Soon after writing the *Letters on the Study and Use of History*, Bolingbroke composed a *Letter on the Spirit of Patriotism* (1736). The defiant opening paragraph declares: "I shall . . . explain myself fully, nor blush to reason on principles that are out of fashion among men, who intend nothing by serving the public."[21] As the author soon proposes "that in order to maintain the moral system of the world"

God gives to all societies a few men of unimpeachable moral virtue, Bolingbroke's subject seems to be morality. For such men to misapply their talents is "the greatest of crimes" since "it is the more incumbent on those" to use their virtue wisely (352–53). Virtue is essential in governors and government to preserve a divinely ordered moral system. At once Bolingbroke applies these remarks to Britain, which has "no profusion of the ethereal spirit" and does not "abound with men of superior genius" (355).

The scene is set. Starting from these assumptions, this brief treatise attempts to stimulate a spirit of patriotism among the younger politicians of the opposition. Once again, Bolingbroke plays down party rancor and portrays an ideal statesman devoted to the welfare of the state, free of self-interest, and given to self-control. Such a statesman's purpose is not merely to display his abundant virtues but to use them to save the constitution from ruin. In contrast, the principal minister and those around him misapply their own talents. Next Bolingbroke posits the typical corrupt minister:

> We will suppose a man imprudent, rash, presumptuous, ungracious, insolent and profligate, in speculation as well as practice. He can bribe, but he cannot seduce: he can buy, but he cannot gain: he can lye, but he cannot deceive. From whence then has such a man his strength? From the general corruption, of the people, nursed up to a full maturity under his administration; from the venality of all orders and all ranks of men, some of whom are so prostitute, that they set themselves to sale, and even prevent application. (356)

This is Bolingbroke's "example" formula, in the language he used repeatedly to denote Walpole. Bolingbroke, however, decides that corruption alone was not enough to supply all Walpole's power; an entirely selfish attitude among the Whigs was essential:

> One party had given their whole attention during several years, to the project of enriching themselves, and impoverishing the rest of the nation; and, by these and other means, of establishing their dominion under the government and with the favor of a family, who were foreigners, and therefore might believe, that they were established on the throne by the good will and strength of this party alone. This party in general were so intent on these views, and many of them, I fear, are so still, that they did not advert in time to the necessary consequences of the measures they abetted: nor did they consider, that the power they raised, and by which

they hoped to govern their country, would govern them with the very rod of iron they forged, and would be the power of a prince or minister, not that of a party long. (356)

The casual phrase, "a prince or minister," suggests indifference, or even equivalence. This passage traces the immediate source of national decline to both Walpole and the king. But Bolingbroke also condemns the Tories for sitting idly, sullenly expecting a savior who never came. Bolingbroke reserves his contempt for the weak and fearful, who nevertheless must be stirred by active leadership into a spirit of opposition. To oppose is "no chimerical, but a real duty," since to oppose is to undertake "The service of our country," "a moral duty" (358). With his customary rhetorical questions, he asks, "To what higher station, to what greater glory can any mortal aspire, than to be, during the whole course of his life, the support of good, the controul of bad government, and the guardian of public liberty?" (359) and so on. He asks what it is to be degraded *voluntarily* from such a position of eminence and public spirit. But he does not stay for an answer. Nor, of course, does his reader. By recognizing what the answer should be, the reader is both "flattered" and also manipulated into accepting the implied answer as right. Having placed patriotism, through such a rhetorical technique, on the highest intellectual and moral plane, Bolingbroke brings in that Augustan favorite, Cato, as an example. Cato's becomes a heroic struggle in defense of liberty against the tyrant Catiline, to whom Walpole had frequently been paralleled in the *Craftsman.* Even if Cato could not finally preserve liberty, he succeeded in prolonging its life (360–62). His example should therefore stimulate the reader to similarly virtuous conduct.

The treatise so far is directed openly at the enemies of liberty, Walpole and his government, with the king never far away. Bolingbroke says his examples are appropriate because, although liberty in contemporary England has the opportunity to flourish, concern for liberty is smaller than ever. His lament is for a state that has wilfully abandoned its chance of establishing liberty; a state where there is "more abject servility" among particular men than he had seen in France; a state where an oligarchy conceals monarchy and where, incredibly, "these cabals, or oligarchies, [are] more respected than majesty itself" (362). What passes for ambition now is "an odd mixture of avarice and vanity" (363). The opposition, Bolingbroke recalls, scented Walpole's blood but thought only of leaping at once into his position and continuing his policies, and therefore lost their chance of removing him. However, Bolingbroke finds consolation in knowing that there are good men, prominent among them Lord Cornbury, to whom the letter is addressed. Cornbury is urged never to slacken the vigil, for "if you cease the combat, you give up the cause" (364) of preserving liberty. Bolingbroke's message is eventually that of the previous decade: "To reform the state therefore is, and ought to be, the object of your opposition" (364).

Not only is eternal policing of a corrupt administration vital; so too is eloquence. Bolingbroke's examples of orators whose eloquence was employed in defense of liberty are Demosthenes and Cicero. Yet rhetoric alone is not sufficient. For Demosthenes to be so effective a patriot, "He must have been master of other arts, subserviently to which his eloquence was employed, and must have had a thorough knowledge of his own state, and of the other states of *Greece*, of their dispositions, and of their interests relatively to their neighbours, . . . he must have possessed an immense fund of knowledge, to make his eloquence in every case successful" (367–68). Similarly, Cicero had perfect knowledge of constitution and government. Kramnick comments that in this essay, "Bolingbroke's description of a good minister reads like the perfect classical orator,"[22] but it is also true that his perfect classical orators have the knowledge and experience of politicians. D. G. James suggested plausibly that Bolingbroke may have had in mind circumstances of Cicero's life, parallel to those of his own, and that he paralleled the argument of the first book of Cicero's *De Oratore.* In this urgent plea for the protection of liberty against corruption, Bolingbroke listens himself to the Roman orator, hero, and defender of liberty.[23]

The examples of Demosthenes and Cicero show that opposition requires all the careful preparation that a rhetorician puts into his eloquence. Liberty is effectively defended by men who blend public spirit, political experience, and rhetorical skill. Like government, opposition must be systematic, "an opposite, but not a dependent system" (370). The final message is that opposition must be constructive, proposing good measures as well as opposing false ones. Bolingbroke saw the weakness of the opposition he had recently left. Wyndham's death in 1740 weakened the opposition further, but when Pulteney capitulated in 1743 it collapsed completely. Bolingbroke's treatise sets out not only the role of a permanent opposition in Parliament, but also the need for effective opponents of corruption to be eloquent, skilled rhetoricians—like himself.

The Idea of a Patriot King

The Idea of a Patriot King has received attention disproportionate to its intrinsic value. This short, lively tract has acquired a reputation for being political philosophy, and has been thought a significant contribution to political theory. In fact, as H. T. Dickinson has recently and rightly argued, the *Idea* is inadequate as practicable theory.[24] As political philosophy the *Idea* is disappointingly superficial. There are, however, two good reasons why it has attracted attention. First, the circumstances of its publication are interesting and controversial. The story has often been told. In brief, Bolingbroke wrote the *Idea* probably in the fall of 1738 and allowed Pope to print a few copies for private circulation. But against Bolingbroke's wishes Pope printed an edition of about fifteen hundred copies in 1739 or 1740. Bolingbroke's private reaction after Pope's death late in 1744 was merely to destroy the remaining copies of Pope's edition; but when extracts began to appear in the *London Magazine* early in 1749, Bolingbroke reacted publicly by issuing his revised "authorized" edition and, in a preface, damning Pope for his treachery.[25] William Warburton, Pope's literary executor and no friend of Bolingbroke, defended the poet's memory and attacked Bolingbroke, who responded in kind with a brief, undistinguished pamphlet.

The other source of attention is the identity of the patriot king. Readers of the *Idea* commonly identify Frederick, Prince of Wales, as the future patriot king and ponder the viability of the treatise and the pragmatic nature of patriot kingship. Dickinson is right to reject the political futility of a scheme that amounts to little more than an exhortation to be virtuous. Yet, although Bolingbroke believed virtue to be essential to the private and the public lives of public men, he was surely not so naive as to think that his treatise proposed a serious political scheme. Instead, the *Idea* is a punitive satire; this accounts for its poverty as practical political theory.

The introduction to the *Idea* sets the work's tone, echoing the *Letter on the Spirit of Patriotism.* The *raison d'être* of this new treatise is the present, corrupt age, the decline of public and private morality, and the erosion of liberty. For all of these Walpole appears to be responsible. In an age of iniquity a spirit of liberty, guided by reason, must take men along the difficult path to virtue; the patriot king will restore the spirit of liberty.

The political system Bolingbroke puts forward is simply limited monarchy: that is, a constitutional monarchy in which power is held jointly by the king, an aristocracy (the House of Lords), and a democracy (the House of Commons). Limited monarchy is, or should be, consistent with liberty. Although Bolingbroke hardly explains his "system" any further, he does say that a patriot king will be necessary to prevent Britain's imminent ruin. Several qualities are expected. A patriot from the earliest possible moment, he must be a man of virtue; but if he does have private vices, he should be able to compensate for them by possessing great public virtues. He should choose his companions and his ministers sensibly, for their moral virtue and ability. Further, the patriot king must promote unity among his people, and he must be popular—as he will be anyway if he is a good king. In short, Bolingbroke suggests: find a virtuous king and Britain's problems are solved! Summarized in this way, the portrait of the patriot king does indeed seem to be simplistic, naive, and unworkable—after all, if the heir to the throne does not turn out like this, the nation cannot legitimately elect an alternative candidate who is. But Bolingbroke had in mind neither Frederick, the heir, nor, perhaps, any workable or constructive philosophy.

The title of the treatise contains an ironic indicator: a "patriot" king, in the political language of the 1730s, would imply a king who supported the "patriot" opposition. The *Craftsman* had established that "patriotism" in the popular language meant opposition to Walpole's ministry. Further, the leading members of the new young generation of opposition politicians were known as the "boy patriots."[26] The assembly of these men around Frederick aligned him with opposition and patriotism, but Frederick's opposition was directed as much against the king as against Walpole. Since the king appointed ministers, once Frederick became king he would, by definition, support not the opposition but the government. A "patriot" king, therefore, can hardly refer to Frederick. Depending on the degree of irony intended in Bolingbroke's statement that "nothing can be more uncommon than a Patriot King" (411), it is possible that the patriot king does not exist at all. On the other hand, Bolingbroke may have modeled his patriot king on the Young Pretender, Charles Edward Stuart, who, in the view of his supporters, was already a king. This identification does not violate the consistency of the *Idea*, but evidence for this is inconclusive.

Bolingbroke states soberly:

I am not wild enough to suppose that a Patriot King can change human nature. But I am reasonable enough to suppose, that, without altering human nature, he may give a check to this course of human affairs, in his own kingdom at least; that he may defeat the designs, and break the spirit of faction, instead of partaking in one, and assuming the other; and that, if he cannot render the union of his subjects universal, he may render it so general as to answer all the ends of good government, private security, public tranquillity, wealth, power, and fame. (412)

Clearly, the designs and the spirit of faction *are* prevalent, and instead of a patriot king, Britain has a king who does partake in the designs and assume the spirit of faction. Bolingbroke goes on, the "great doctors in politics . . . must be very obstinate indeed, if they refuse to acknowledge, that a wise and good prince can unite a divided people, though a weak and wicked prince cannot" (413). Further, "the consequences of national union are glory and happiness to the prince and the people; whilst those of disunion bring shame and misery on both" (413). In the light of Bolingbroke's repeated view that Britain is divided, the implication is that "a weak and wicked prince" sits on the throne. The next paragraph confirms that these remarks apply to contemporary Britain. Britain experiences "the unexampled avowal of contrary principles. Hitherto it has been thought the highest pitch of profligacy is to own, instead of concealing, crimes; and to take pride in them, instead of being ashamed of them. But in our age men have soared to a pitch still higher. . . . The men I speak of contend, that it is not enough to be vicious by practice and habit, but that it is necessary to be so by principle" (413). This attitude was expressed by Pope in 1738 (when Bolingbroke was probably writing the *Idea*): "Not to be corrupted is the shame."[27]

As the first of these three paragraphs speaks of good and bad monarchs, so the third returns to "A king who esteems it his duty to support, or to restore, if that be needful, the free constitution of a limited monarchy; who forms and maintains a wise and good administration; who subdues faction, and promotes the union of his people: and who makes their greatest good the constant object of his government" (414). The three paragraphs suggest that it is indeed almost impossible to find a true patriot king, but that without doubt

Britain in the late 1730s possesses a king who presides over a divided, corrupt, shameful nation. To be sure, George is not a king who has the interests described in that third paragraph.

In contrast, the first quality to look for in a king or his chosen ministers is virtue. Bolingbroke states that he would prefer virtue to be real, not assumed. Merely by drawing this distinction, he implies that at the time of writing he has some reason to think that virtue in public life is assumed rather than real. Similarly, at the beginning of the treatise, it would not be Bolingbroke's fault if kings "are not always held divine, and their persons always sacred" (378); irony suggests that the present king is *not* revered, no doubt with good reason. Bolingbroke concentrates upon several other issues in ways that serve the same function as rhetorical questions. A patriot king does not abet party or faction, he says; but who ever suggested that kings do? Factions "can never create any obstruction to a prince who pursues the union of his subjects, nor disturb the peace of his government" (410), but Bolingbroke implies that the present king does not pursue such a high end as the union of his subjects. The *Idea* contrasts the patriot king's laudable conduct with George II's encouragement of corruption.

All the patriot king's actions are postulated as occurring at some time in the future, and the total decline of Britain is repeatedly reintroduced to suggest that the decline is the present king's fault: George has chosen weak and wicked ministers, and he has unsavory companions in his private life. It is his fault that British merchant ships are continually subjected to acts of Spanish piracy, and so on. In all Bolingbroke identifies the grand source of corruption as no longer Walpole, but George II, who commands no respect and would be a tyrant if given the chance. He is living proof that "a divine right to govern ill, is an absurdity, to assert it blasphemy" (379); or as Pope put it, Dullness's reign flourishes as long as one doctrine is propagated: "The RIGHT DIVINE of Kings to govern wrong."[28] An anonymous pamphleteer, attacking Bolingbroke's rhetoric and dismantling the *Idea* as political theory, accurately called the patriot king "a mock *Monarch* in the Clouds."[29] This ideal king should support the principle of the present opposition, but George II resists a popular and just opposition. *The Idea of a Patriot King* is a punitive satire on King George, the would-be tyrant who destroys the value of British life.

Chapter Six

The Philosophical Works

David Mallet's edition of Bolingbroke's *Works* in five substantial volumes was published on 6 March 1754. The previously unpublished material consisted of two early, insignificant pieces, "A Letter occasioned by one of Archbishop Tillotson's Sermons," and "The Substance of some Letters to M. Pouilly," four long letters, or essays, addressed to Pope, and eighty-one "Fragments, or Minutes of Essays." All these were also published separately by Bowyer and Strahan as Bolingbroke's *Philosophical Works* in June 1754. As the fury against the *Letters on the Study and Use of History* was beginning to abate, these new works provoked another raging torrent against Bolingbroke's memory. In little more than two years, ten authors, again mostly learned clergymen, had reviled the deistic or atheistic tendency of these writings.

The four letters to Pope contain a discussion of the "nature, extent, and reality of human knowledge" (the most interesting and least prejudiced of the four), a demolition job on "unreasoning" philosophy, a treatise on the rise of monotheism, and a lengthy attack on the authority of the church. These four are preceded by an introductory letter to Pope that had attracted very little critical attention when published the previous year.[1] This introductory letter touches on some of the "public" concerns of Pope's poetry, warns the poet that he will be opposed by stronger powers than the common herd of scribblers, and asserts Bolingbroke's belief in the moral function of poetry. In this letter Bolingbroke defines the subject of the four letters to Pope: "first philosophy," that is, "that which deserves the first place on account of the dignity, and importance of its objects, 'natural theology or theism, and natural religion or ethics.' "[2] Natural philosophy is placed first because contemplation of nature ("by which I mean the whole system of God's works, as far as it lies open to us") is the fountain of all sciences, as well as of ethics and theology (3:50).

In the "Fragments, or Minutes of Essays"—in fact a continuous, but disorganized, prose treatise—Bolingbroke discusses a reasonably wide range of philosophical topics, notably the nature of God, of ideas, and of the law of nature; the moral nature of man and the will of God; religious and theological doctrines, revelation, the origins of civil society, the origin of evil, the dispensations of Providence, free will, and the immortality of the soul. Bolingbroke emerges from these discussions as a fierce critic of the clergy, and an equally fierce proponent of the idea that the earth was not created for man, but is only a small part of an infinite universe. He also demonstrates his contempt for Plato and his followers, among many other philosophers whom he dismisses at length as propagators of "fantastical knowledge."

The general consensus since 1754 has been that these are the dull writings of a second-rate philosopher. It has also been assumed that philosophy was, for Bolingbroke, some kind of substitute for politics or political writing. But apart from the introductory letter to Pope (written possibly as early as 1738), these philosophical writings were written *before* Bolingbroke's political career was over, and only revised afterwards.

Bolingbroke says in a prefatory statement that the "Fragments" and the letters to Pope "are all nothing more than repetitions of conversations often interrupted, often renewed, and often carried on a little confusedly" (4:111). I am not concerned here with questions of influence, but with the nature of Bolingbroke's philosophical writings. They are neither truly conversational, as that prefatory remark might suggest, nor formal. The philosophical works together constitute a bulk of such formidable length that they discourage detailed analysis—if indeed that were desirable. This chapter, seeking to do no more than identify some of the principal characteristics of Bolingbroke's rhetorical style in these writings, makes no attempt to analyze his philosophy.

Letters, or Essays, addressed to Alexander Pope

Several tendencies of the four letters to Pope stand out: Bolingbroke's deism, his insistence that the earth was not made for man, his reliance on the guiding power of reason, and his dismissal of generations of philosophers, however revered.[3]

In the first essay Bolingbroke tries to identify the real and the natural, and to distinguish them from the imaginary and the artificial, to find truth and distinguish it from error. These noble and disinterested aims are not achieved by means of any rigorous scholarship, nor is there very much evidence of consistent or foolproof logic. For example, one passage condemns Plato, who frequently comes under attack, on the grounds that he speaks

> of demons, that is, of invisible spiritual natures: but of these he confesses himself unable to speak on the strength of his parts, or on his own knowledge; for which reason he has recourse to tradition, and to the authority of the ancients, who were born of gods, and knew their parents extremely well. . . . These men we must believe, he says, though the things they have delivered down be not confirmed by conclusive nor even by probable reasons. . . . On such respectable authority did the divine Plato vend, to his own and to future ages, all the mysterious nonsense that Pythagoras and he had imported from the Egyptian and Eastern schools of theology and philosophy. (3:179)

This may be splendid sarcastic rhetoric, but it is somewhat unfair condemnation, since Bolingbroke himself is content to accept the authority of equally dubious sources. Although in his philosophical writings Bolingbroke "constantly rejected the value of the *a priori* method of reasoning, he was frequently guilty of adopting it" himself,[4] and although he was guilty of other such inconsistencies, he did articulate some valuable arguments and principles. In his philosophical works as in his political analysis, even if Bolingbroke cannot provide a plausibly argued alternative, he knows what to condemn. From Plato to Malebranche and Berkeley, philosophers who have adopted a priori reasoning, Bolingbroke says, "have done all that human capacity can do in a wrong method; but all they have done has been to vend us poetry for philosophy, and to multiply systems of imagination" (3:71). Like imagination in philosophy, superstition has been the foundation on which ancient religions have been based (3:137). From here Bolingbroke returns to poetry and philosophy: "Hesiod, and your Homer, and others more ancient than either, had filled the world with demons and genii: and as poets were the philosophers of those ages among the Greeks, the machinery of poetry soon came to be that of philosophy. Plato, as great a poet as any of them in the garb of a philosopher, multiplied vastly these imaginary beings, and assigned them different ranks and different employments" (3:138). The "poetic"—that part of philosophers' thoughts dominated by imagination—leads to superstition, error, oppression, and falsehood (3:163–64).

Just as imagination may replace reason as the mistaken philosopher's guide, so passion may replace reason. Bolingbroke suggests that "the first missionaries," confronted by "people immersed in ignorance and superstition" (3:222), exploited

> a multitude, in whom appetites and prepossessions, affections and passions, raised by sensible objects, were strong, and the force of reason small. It was necessary therefore, in the opinion of these missionaries of good policy and good manners, and, in order to promote them both, of religion likewise, to suit their doctrines to such gross conceptions, and to raise such affections and passions by human images, and by objects that made strong impressions on sense, as might be opposed with success to such as were raised by human images, and by sensible objects too, and were destructive of order, and pernicious to society. (3:224)

Erroneous philosophy, not founded on reason, has thus led men away from the truth and toward chaos.

One of Bolingbroke's key distinctions in his discussion of misleading philosophy is that between philosophy and poetry. Homer, Bolingbroke thought, never intended the *Iliad* to be a philosophical poem: Homer wrote a poem "meant to flatter his countrymen, by recording the feats of his ancestors" (3:235) and peopled his narrative with gods simply drawn from "the theology of his age." In the same way, Tasso, Milton, and even Pope in *The Rape of the Lock*, select the "machinery" of gods, and so on, for their own poetic purposes. It is madness to attribute "philosophy" to these authors on the evidence of their poems. Continuing this discussion later, Bolingbroke remarks that Plato "was much more a poetical philosopher than Homer was a philosophical poet" (3:294) and that he has done more damage to philosophy than Homer ever could. Undesirable as it may be, there is a marriage of poetry and philosophy, as is clear from yet another of Bolingbroke's attacks on Plato: "Among these gross errors there is scarce any more gross, or of more extensive influence, than this that supposes a power in the mind, which the mind has not, and the reality of ideas of general natures, though these cannot exist abstractedly from particulars" (3:126). Despite the opposition of Bacon, Descartes, and Locke, "the field of knowledge . . . may be therefore over-run again by a new crop springing from old roots that they neglected to grub or helped to preserve" (3:126–27). The "lofty madness" of Plato may, with Aristotle's "pompous jargon," regain a hold, as metaphysics begins to reassert itself, bringing about an irrational perception of the world: "All this may happen, and if dulness should re-establish her empire in poetry, whilst that of madness is restored in philosophy, how glorious an age may the next become, when all the defects, and all the follies of this are complete? Once more, all this may happen" (3:127).

This is followed by a curious passage, apparently about Queen Caroline, who

> interests herself in nice and subtile disputations about space: from metaphysics she rises to theology. She attends frequently to the controversy, . . . about that profound mystery the Trinity. She studies with much application the 'analogy of revealed religion to the constitution and course of nature.'—She understands the whole argument perfectly, and concludes, with the right reverend author, that it is not 'so clear a case that there is nothing in revealed religion.' Such royal, such lucrative encouragement must needs keep both metaphysics and the sublimest theology in credit; . . . let what has been here said stand for one example of the arts employed by the mind to enlarge its knowledge, and to let it serve to show how these arts degenerate into artifice, deceive even the mind that invented them, and, instead of enlarging knowledge, enlarge and multiply error. (3:127)

The queen's interest in theology, and her patronage of theologians, remained something of a public joke until her death in 1737. Her "lucrative encouragement" might also suggest Caroline's much-maligned patronage of Stephen Duck, the thresher-poet: is it possible that the *Dunciad*'s empire of dullness is presided over by Caroline? that she is herself Pope's Queen Dulness?[5] Whatever the answer to that speculation, the decline of poetry and the decay of philosophy take place together.

In an important statement about the nature of philosophical writing, in contrast with poetry, Bolingbroke says that his own writing must be subordinate to truth and reason; an argument is essential (whereas a poem need not contain one), and a philosopher must not, like Plato, address only the imagination. "There is no need however to banish eloquence out of philosophy; and truth and reason are no enemies to the purity, nor to the ornaments of language. . . . the business of the philosopher is to dilate, if I may borrow this word from Tully [i.e., Cicero], to press, to prove, to convince; and that of the poet to hint, to touch his subject with short and spirited strokes, to warm the affections, and to speak to the heart" (3:44). The business of the philosopher is, therefore, to achieve the usual aims of rhetoric: "to press, to prove, to convince." In making this point, Bolingbroke uses the simple rhetorical device of appealing to an ancient authority: Cicero. This emphasis on the rhetoric of the philosopher is repeated later when he says "of rhetoric in general, the practice of which I esteem much, the theory little, that it applies images, framed or borrowed by imagination, to ideas and notions which are framed by judgment, so as to warm the affections, to move the passions, and to determine the will; so as to assist nature, not to oppress her" (3:128). But the reader thinking that rhetoric is the domain of philosophy now finds that the distinction between philosophy and poetry is, after all, not so great, since both poetry and rhetoric "warm the affections." In fact, "the tribe nearest allied" to poets is that of "orators."

Bolingbroke has much to say about rhetorical figures, allegory, fables, and satirical devices. Rhetoric, he knows, may be abused, "But if rhetoric were banished out of the world, and logic with it, eloquence and reason would still remain" (3:130); and figures in philosophical writing ought to be like varnish on a canvas, "not to be used to alter the intellectual picture" but "to give a greater lustre, and to make it better seen" (3:134). Finally, Bolingbroke suggests that "Allusion, allegory, metaphor, and every part of figurative style is the poet's language. Figments of imagination are his subject. The philosopher may sometimes employ the former cautiously, and under much control: the latter never. Reason must be his guide, and truth alone his subject" (3:306). And he observes that "nothing could be more proper, nor effectual, to promote fantastical knowledge, than a method of philosophising by fables, symbols, and almost a perpetual allegory" (3:434). Even when he discusses rhetoric, Bolingbroke employs it himself. As we should perhaps expect of a political rhetorician's writing, these essays recommend their author as a philosopher whose guide is reason, his subject truth, his writing uncontaminated by imagination or superstition.

Fragments, or Minutes of Essays

In the *Fragments, or Minutes of Essays* Bolingbroke attacks priestcraft for many reasons, one of which is the pretense of revelation: "The mischief lies in the way of proof. Reason establishes the belief of an all-perfect Being. Revelation supposes it. If we impute any imperfection to this Being, we shake the belief of him. The imputation implies contradiction, and reason is set in opposition to reason. But, on the other hand, some things may be admitted piously, on the faith of a revelation, concerning which we can scarce attempt to reason without impiety" (4:438). Elsewhere he says that any revelation would be consistent with the first revelation: that is, it would accord with what reason would expect (4:475–77). Although less extreme than Hobbes's skepticism, Bolingbroke's argument points in the same direction. In the *Fragments* Bolingbroke dissociates himself from Hobbes (among other philosophers): "I cannot soar so high as Plato and Cudworth. I will not sink so low as Protagoras, and other ancients; as Hobbes, and other moderns. The former amaze, instead of instructing me; and if I understand the latter, I only understand them, to know that they impose on themselves, and would impose on me, the grossest absurdities. Strange extremes!" (4:119). The effect of this passage is not so much to dissociate Bolingbroke from Hobbes particularly, but from any philosopher whom he considers extreme. This dissociation has the rhetorical function of placing Bolingbroke in a middle position where readers are likely to associate him with moderation, or in a later passage, with sober judgment: "We are apt to carry the judgments we make into extremes, and the characters we give into panegyrics or satyrs" (4:328). What is more important, once Bolingbroke is associated with such a position, he can exploit the association to ally himself with truth, since "There is a middle point between these extremes, where the truth lies: and he who seeks it may find it" (4:329). Once it is established that moderation, truth, and Bolingbroke are all to be found somewhere in the middle between extremes, Bolingbroke's judgments are rhetorically more convincing. For instance, by means of a rhetorical question, he once again places himself between the extremes of Plato and Hobbes, in order to propagate his own view: "How preferable is the middle opinion between these two extremes, that God instituted moral obligations when he made moral agents, that the law of their nature is the law of his will, and that, how indifferent soever we may presume every thing is to him before his will has determined it to be, it becomes, after this determination, a necessary, though created nature?" (4:406).

In these essays Bolingbroke generally appeals to sober reason by such means as these. But his rhetoric is not devoted only to self-presentation. The opening of Fragment III seeks to expose an absurdity by analogy:

If any man should advance, that we ought to proceed on the known principles of mathematics, not because there are such in nature, but because mathematicians have made an agreement or compact to proceed upon them as if there were such, I suspect that he would be esteemed mad. What then were Hobbes, his predecessors, and his successors, who affirmed that all distinction between moral good and evil, just and unjust, is established solely by institution: and that our moral obligations are derived from the laws of society, not from the law of nature? This extravagant system has been over and over refuted by many writers of our own and other countries. (4:145)

Bolingbroke's analogy is unjust because like is not compared with like. Only a fool, however, would disagree with the opening proposition, and only a fool would trouble even to answer the question that follows. By using the analogy, therefore, Bolingbroke ensures that the reader approves this condemnation of an "extravagant" system. This technique recurs in the *Fragments*. Only the convinced Pythagorean is indignant—or unwise—enough to answer the charge that Pythagoras "inveloped his doctrines in mystery to make them pass for divine, laid the foundations of them out of the ken of human reason, and acquired a great reputation in metaphysics and divine philosophy, by the usual method, by not being understood" (4:273). No one argues against sarcasm like that without laying himself open to attack.

Part of Bolingbroke's destruction of Samuel Clarke's theological arguments casts doubt enough on Clarke's conclusions, but Bolingbroke also undermines Clarke's logic with a casual phrase such as "Having assumed, which he calls proving, . . ." (4:302). Now, no one doubts that assumption is no substitute for proof, and Bolingbroke repeats "having assumed all this, I say, he proceeds to argue in this manner," so that the reader will come to Clarke's argument with a disinclination (however slight) to believe that Clarke can be right.

This strategy is common in Bolingbroke's philosophical writing. He could never change his character as a polemicist. His attack on metaphysicians, therefore, relies for its success on the reader's accepting Bolingbroke's intellectual superiority: "Metaphysical writers counsel us sometimes very gravely to silence imagination, that we may attend to experience, and hearken to the voice of reason. The advice is good, and they would neither puzzle themselves, nor perplex knowledge, if they took it as they give it. But who can forbear smiling, when these very men abandon themselves, at the same instant, to all the seductions and to all the transports of their own imaginations?" (4:439). Presumably, Bolingbroke expects his reader also not to "forbear smiling": if so, the reader is, in a way, flattered into thinking of himself as standing on the same intellectual level as the author. The reader needs to extend this to a sort of moral superiority if he is to approve of this condemnation of the clergy: "The principal and most effectual weapon, which the clergy employed to make men submit to this tyranny, was the chimerical weapon of excommunication, forged in the chimerical fire of hell" (4:486). The repetition of "chimerical" and the association of the clergy with hell are sufficient pointers to Bolingbroke's strictures on the tyranny of the church: anyone wishing to counter this must accept the burden of proof.

The frequent interpolations of personal comments to Pope emphasize the supposed informality of the essays and of their origin in conversation. When Bolingbroke tells Pope: "If you improve in your own thoughts the hints dispersed in the precedent reflections, you, whose good understanding is undebauched by metaphysics, will see very evidently the truth of these two propositions" (4:374), the reader almost overhears a conversation. Although Bolingbroke adopts no persona in these works, he does adopt an implied reader, as in this passage. Only if we consciously remember that "you" is Pope (for there is no more explicit identification here) do we refrain from placing ourselves in the position of addressee.

On 14 December 1725 Bolingbroke made a revealing statement about philosophy; having told Swift that "Pope and you are very great wits, and I think you very indifferent Philosophers," he goes on to discuss Swift's definition of man: "Your Definition of Animal capax Rationis instead of the Common one Animal Rationale, will not bear examination. define but Reason, and you will see why your distinction is no better than that of the Pontiffe Cotta beween mala Ratio and bona Ratio. But enough of this. make us a visit and I'le subscribe to any side of these important Questions which you please."[6] The last sentence reveals that Bolingbroke thinks his role in philosophy is to debate—predominantly an oral activity. And like a truly dispassionate debater, he does not care which side of the question he supports. It is not too fanciful to picture Bolingbroke, in those many conversations with Pope, simply arguing and speculating in metaphysics for the love of it, paying as much attention to his own eloquence as to his argument.

Bolingbroke claimed that "The opinions I held are exposed as clearly, as they ought to be by a man who thinks his opinions founded in truth. I thought, and I think still, that mine were so" (4:111). But these philosophical works were rapidly denounced as, among other things, insincere. Thomas Hayter's judgment, in 1754, was typical, if overstated. Hayter thought Bolingbroke "left his posthumous Works to infatuate the Nation which he had not the Pleasure to ruin" and condemned a "Book, written with a View to pull up the Root of all human Society."[7] John Hill seems to have gone so far as to pay for the printing of his refutation of Bolingbroke's philosophy:[8] Hill must have been wealthy or foolhardy to publish over six hundred pages of argument no different in substance from any of the others that appeared in 1754 or 1755, such as Ralph Heathcote's effort to "prevent the dreadful effects, which so pernicious a Collection was likely to have upon the Public."[9] Thomas Randolph's *Certainty of a Future State* (Oxford, 1755) suggested that Bolingbroke's *Works* were subversive of all religion, and George Anderson devoted four hundred and fifty pages to "all the blunders, all the errors, all the immorality, all the impiety, and all the Atheism, that I find in Lord BOLINGBROKE'S philosophical works, and for all the disservice they are calculated to do mankind."[10] Charles Bulkley and John Leland added their sober voices to the furor, and William Warburton took the opportunity to defend his slighted friend Pope by publishing a prejudiced attack on Bolingbroke's philosophy. Most of these hostile works took Bolingbroke to task for his outright attack on organized religion, usually seeking to demonstrate that his arguments were superficial, his logic faulty, and his appeal "merely" rhetorical. Bolingbroke's reputation as a philosopher has scarcely recovered.

Chapter Seven

Bolingbroke and His Literary Milieu

As the chief architect of the opposition Bolingbroke quickly developed a mere attempt to oust Walpole from office into a campaign designed to arrest the rapid moral decline of British society. His political language, expressed chiefly in the *Craftsman* until 1736, was evidently the language of the opposition. It was Bolingbroke who in that periodical began to associate opposition with "patriotism" and "virtue," two catchwords that became as prominent in the political vocabulary as the ironic "great man." These examples typified Bolingbroke's originally rhetorical devices that simply passed into the stock opposition vocabulary, to be expanded and developed later in *The Idea of a Patriot King.*

Pope and Gay, no political thinkers, employ this stock vocabulary when it suits their satiric intentions. Kramnick suggests reasonably that Pope's *One Thousand Seven Hundred and Forty*—self-evidently topical, political, and disenchanted—versifies ideas from the *Patriot King.*[1] Similarly, Gay's *Fables* (second series) gain much of their political impetus from the opposition vocabulary;[2] one fable in particular (2, vi) puts forward one of Bolingbroke's stock arguments about a minister who tries to keep people away from the king. Sven Armens suggests that Gay derived his political views from those later articulated in the *Patriot King*, but Kramnick counters that Gay simply recited stock opposition attitudes[3]—Gay was responding to views obtained from Bolingbroke, without necessarily borrowing exactly from Bolingbroke's writings. In much the same way, Pope's "politicizing" of the 1743 *Dunciad* is indebted to the vocabulary and the general political stance of Bolingbroke and the *Craftsman.*[4]

Thus, in the writings of others, an emphasis on virtue, or patriotism, or a great man, does not necessarily indicate a conscious borrowing from Bolingbroke, nor even from the *Craftsman*, but it usually does indicate conscious participation in Bolingbroke's opposition. His "influence" on his friends' work is not usually found in verbal echoes, but more generally in his political ideas, originating perhaps in his conversation. He is the only genuine political thinker among them.

Bolingbroke was the dominant political thinker in the group of authors who exploited the rhetoric of "virtue" in the 1730s. Mabel H. Cable has indicated the main "opposition" literature that sprang up in the late 1730s around the idea of a patriot king: James Thomson's *Liberty* (1735–36) and *Edward and Eleonora* (1739), Richard Glover's *Leonidas* (1737), David Mallet's *Mustapha* (1739), and Henry Brooke's *Gustavus Vasa* (1739). This neglected literature, says Cable, "is chiefly rhetoric; perhaps it is nothing more."[5] More significant than any of these works is Pope's *Epistle to Augustus* (1737). Both this poem and Bolingbroke's essays in the *Craftsman* (particularly the *Remarks on the History of England*) establish "virtue" as a quality requisite for good ministers and good kings. By ironic implication, virtue becomes the property of those who oppose bad ministers and bad kings. At about the time Bolingbroke was developing this idea of virtue in his portrait of the patriot king, Pope participated most explicitly in Bolingbroke's rhetoric of virtue in the *Epilogue to the Satires, Dialogue I* (1738). Surveying the state of the nation, Pope gloomily announces that vice now

> sees pale Virtue carted in her Stead!
> Lo! at the Wheels of her Triumphal Car,
> Old *England's* Genius, rough with many a Scar,
> Dragg'd in the Dust! his Arms hang idly round,
> His Flag inverted trails along the ground!
> Our Youth, all liv'ry'd o'er with foreign Gold,
> Before her dance; behind her crawl the Old!
> See thronging Millions to the Pagod run,
> And offer Country, Parent, Wife, or Son!
> Hear her black Trumpet thro' the Land proclaim,
> That 'Not to be corrupted is the Shame.'
> In Soldier, Churchman, Patriot, Man in Pow'r,
> 'Tis Avarice all, Ambition is no more!
> See, all our Nobles begging to be Slaves!
> See, all our Fools aspiring to be Knaves! (150–64)

Like this poem, Bolingbroke's *Dissertation upon Parties* (1733–34) presents a vision of Britain in which virtue and vice have changed places, morality has been replaced by immorality, avarice dominates, and "many noblemen and gentlemen debase themselves to [the] meanness" of "the meanest grubs on earth."[6] Like Bolingbroke and the patriots, Pope loftily declares at the end of his poem: "Yet may this Verse (if such a Verse remain) / Show there was one who held it in disdain" (171–72).

Although revealing little about "influence," alignments between Bolingbroke's political attitude and Pope's, like the rhetoric of examples, present evidence that Bolingbroke and Pope share one, coherent moral vision. Swift's work likewise reveals several attitudes associated with Bolingbroke's thinking. The King of Brobdingnag, it is sometimes suggested, is a patriot king.[7] Among Swift's less obvious work, the poem "A Libel on D— D—. And A Certain Great Lord" (1730) disapproves of Walpole's "more than R[oya]l Will," a subject disapproved not only in numerous miscellaneous issues of the *Craftsman*, but as a central point in Bolingbroke's *Remarks on the History of England.* Similarly, Swift's poem "To Mr Gay" (1731?) recalls Bolingbroke's account of Caleb D'Anvers's steward in the West Indies.[8] In addition, Swift and Bolingbroke shared many conceptions about the nature, use, and value of history.

There is no doubt that the Augustans participated together in a crusade against degeneracy and corruption in George II's Britain, a concerted effort to resist the forces that could "make ONE MIGHTY DUNCIAD OF THE LAND."[9] Bolingbroke sees the decline of Britain in Pope's terms: "if dulness should re-establish her empire in poetry, whilst that of madness is restored in philosophy, how glorious an age may the next become, when all the defects, and all the follies of this are complete?"[10] Or perhaps Pope sees it in Bolingbroke's terms:

> *Philosophy*, that lean'd on Heav'n before,
> Shrinks to her second cause, and is no more.
> *Physic* of *Metaphysic* begs defence,
> And *Metaphysic* calls for aid on Sense![11]

Bolingbroke had given dullness a specifically political connotation in the Dedication to *A Dissertation upon Parties* in 1735. With a Gulliverian shift of perspective, Bolingbroke introduces Walpole:

> The minister, who grows less by his elevation, like a little statue placed on a mighty pedestal, will always have this jealousy strong about him.

He must of course select a faction to himself; and this faction must be composed, to answer his purposes, of men servilely obsequious, or extremely inferior to him by their talents. Whenever this happens, the reign of venality, of prostitution, of ignorance, of futility, and of dulness commences.[12]

Bolingbroke's thesis that dullness, together with wider moral depravity, is a consequence of Walpole's corrupt administration, as it would be of any corrupt administration, is evident also in the increased political implication of Pope's revised *Dunciad*.

Paralleling George's increasing unpopularity in the nation at large, one tendency of Pope's poetry in the 1730s and in the 1743 *Dunciad* is increasingly open hostility to the monarch and the monarchy. Bolingbroke's writing displays the same tendency to mirror public opinion of the king: his *Craftsman* essays, carefully excluding George at first, gradually begin to attack him as well as Walpole. Indeed, as Maynard Mack has recently made known, the Arch Dunce of the 1728 *Dunciad* might originally have been George II.[13] But, cautiously perhaps, Pope rejected the relevant passages before publication, allowing his unrestrained hostility to the king to emerge only later.[14] The sustained satire in which Pope does openly attack George is, of course, the *Epistle to Augustus*, whose assessment of the king is close to—perhaps derived from—Bolingbroke's satire of George in the *Idea of a Patriot King*.

As Bolingbroke is the central political thinker in the group assembled around him, so he is the central philosophical figure. As Louis Bredvold says, even "Pope's *Essay on Man* . . . and Bolingbroke's philosophical excursions, were speculations of a kind not common among [the satirists]."[15] Also, as Bredvold notes, Swift was quite surprised by the *Essay*: "I confess I did never imagine you were so deep in Morals," he told Pope, who seems to have been mildly embarrassed by his own excursions into philosophy: "I have only one piece of mercy to beg of you," he wrote to Swift, "do not laugh at my gravity, but permit me to wear the beard of a philosopher, till I pull it off, and make a jest of it myself. 'Tis just what my Lord Bolingbroke is doing with Metaphysicks."[16] Bolingbroke himself was never as bashful. If philosophy was an unusual subject for Pope, it was not so for Bolingbroke, who had been accustomed to philosophical discussion since his first spell in France. *An Essay on Man* owes some of its philosophical content to the conversation, but probably not to any of the published writing, of Bolingbroke, and the poem may well owe some of its rhetorical structure to Bolingbroke's conception of literature.[17]

Bolingbroke's friends thought of him as a fine philosopher and a finer writer. Swift was convinced that Bolingbroke's metaphysical writings would prove "a glorious undertaking" and Pope thought Bolingbroke would "be more known to posterity as a writer and philosopher than as a statesman."[18] Swift and Pope were impressed by their friend's political writing, too: Swift judged the *Dissertation* "masterly written" and Pope "spoke very highly of [Bolingbroke's] dissertation on the English history, and that on parties, and called him 'absolutely the best writer of the age.' "[19] Reading the *Letters on the Study and Use of History*, Pope was moved to conclude that nothing could "depress" Bolingbroke's "genius" and to make yet another statement about his friend's greatness.[20] These political and historical writings, not the philosophical works, have won Bolingbroke almost all his acclaim.

As statesman and controversialist, Bolingbroke enjoyed a high reputation for his oratorical skills; as writer, he was praised for his style. Among his contemporaries only James Hervey took exception to "the popular Notion" that Bolingbroke's "*Style* is so correct, elegant, and noble, as to be a *Standard* for *fine Writing*."[21] One interesting judgment was that of Hugh Blair: "the Style that runs through all of [Bolingbroke's] political writings, is that of one declaiming with heat, rather than writing with deliberation." Bolingbroke's method, Blair thought, "is allowable, and graceful in an Orator," but perhaps not in a writer.[22] Bolingbroke's friends valued his writing—and his conversation—for its style as well as for its ideas. Chesterfield hinted that Bolingbroke's style is equally apt for speech and writing: "The late Lord Bolingbroke, without the least trouble, talked all day long full as elegantly as he wrote. Why? Not by a peculiar gift from heaven; but, as he has often told me himself, by an early and constant attention to his style."[23] In terms that seem to justify Blair's judgment, Chesterfield advised his son to use Bolingbroke's writings:

> Having mentioned Lord Bolingbroke's style, which is, undoubtedly, infinitely superior to anybody's, I would have you read his works, which you have, over and over again, with particular attention to his style. Transcribe, imitate, emulate it, if possible; that would be of real use to

you in the House of Commons, in negotiations, in conversation; with that, you may justly hope to please, to persuade, to seduce, to impose;[24]

or, in other words, to control an audience. Chesterfield clearly conceived of Bolingbroke's celebrated style as a versatile, refined rhetorical instrument.

This study has emphasized Bolingbroke's "style," something definable as his rhetoric. Bolingbroke's rhetoric is a technique designed to persuade his audience to accept his assessment of a disordered world governed by self-interest, greed, and corrupt mismanagement. Underpinned by a coherent conception of a desperately needed morality, Bolingbroke's vision of the whole political and cultural milieu reappears in the work of the Augustan satirists; his vision is transformed by Pope and Swift into their most enduring satires. The members of Bolingbroke's circle thought of Bolingbroke as a great thinker and writer to whom they should defer. Contemporary commentators may have thought of Pope as the foremost poet, of Swift as the foremost pamphleteer, but it was neither Pope nor Swift, but Bolingbroke whom Walpole opposed to the extent of spending £50,000 on subsidies for newspapers.[25] Bolingbroke was the leader, the artful persuader whose eloquence spelled danger for his adversary. Bolingbroke's writing not only makes important contributions to political science and historiography, but is also valuable for its rhetoric. Even if we disagree with Pope's judgment that Bolingbroke was " 'absolutely the best writer of the age,' " Bolingbroke's writing deserves our serious attention.

Notes and References

Chapter One

1. Jonathan Swift, *Journal to Stella*, ed. Harold Williams (Oxford: Clarendon Press, 1948), 2:495.

2. 17 November 1726; *The Letters of John Gay*, ed. C. F. Burgess (Oxford: Clarendon Press, 1966), p. 60.

3. *The Correspondence of Alexander Pope*, ed. George Sherburn (Oxford, 1956), 4:153.

4. H. T. Dickinson, *Bolingbroke* (London, 1970), pp. 2–3.

5. Ibid., p. 37.

6. E.g., William Stratford to Edward Harley, 18 July 1711, *Historical Manuscripts Commission, Portland MSS* (London, 1901), 7:39.

7. Dickinson, *Bolingbroke*, pp. 38, 42.

8. 6 November 1708; *Historical Manuscripts Commission, Bath MSS* (London, 1904), 1:193.

9. Dickinson, p. 59, and Geoffrey Holmes, "Harley, St. John and the Death of the Tory Party," in *Britain after the Glorious Revolution 1689–1714*, ed. Geoffrey Holmes (London, 1969), p. 219.

10. Dickinson, *Bolingbroke*, pp. 64–65, and Holmes, "Harley, St. John . . . ," p. 219.

11. Holmes, "Harley, St. John . . . ," pp. 220–21.

12. Cf. H. T. Dickinson, "The Attempt to Assassinate Harley, 1711," *History Today* 15 (1965):788–95.

13. Dickinson, *Bolingbroke*, p. 77.

14. Holmes, "Harley, St. John . . . ," p. 222. See also Dickinson, "The October Club," *Huntington Library Quarterly* 33 (1969–70):155–73.

15. *Works*, 1:117.

16. See J. A. Downie, *Robert Harley and the Press: Propaganda and Public Opinion in the Age of Swift and Defoe* (Cambridge, 1979).

17. Bolingbroke at least read the proofs (*The Correspondence of Jonathan Swift*, ed. Harold Williams [Oxford, 1963–65], 1:272). Cf. J. A. Downie, "*The Conduct of the Allies*: The Question of Influence," in *The Art of Jonathan Swift*, ed. Clive T. Probyn (London: Vision Press, 1978), pp. 108–28.

18. Dickinson, *Bolingbroke*, p. 89.

19. A. D. MacLachlan, "The Road to Peace 1710–13," in Holmes, *Britain after the Glorious Revolution*, pp. 210–11.

20. Isaac Kramnick, *Bolingbroke and His Circle: The Politics of Nostalgia in the Age of Walpole* (Cambridge, Mass., 1968), p. 12.

21. Dickinson, *Bolingbroke*, p. 116.

22. See Bolingbroke's *Letter to Sir William Windham*, in *Works*, 1:111–79.

23. Dickinson, *Bolingbroke*, p. 146.

24. Cf. Kenneth Woodbridge, "Bolingbroke's Château of La Source," *Garden History* 4, no. 3 (Autumn 1976):50–64.

25. Dickinson, *Bolingbroke*, p. 156.

26. Kramnick, *Bolingbroke*, p. 16.

27. E. R. Briggs, "The Political Academies of France in the Early 18th Century, with Special Reference to the Clubs [*sic*] de l'Entresol, and to its Founder, the Abbé Pierre-Joseph Alary," Ph.D. dissertation (Cambridge University, 1931), pp. 82–144.

28. Ibid., p. 174.

29. To his father, 12 August 1720; British Library, Additional MSS 34,196, fol. 13^{v}. See also Bolingbroke to Swift, 17 March 1719, in Swift, *Correspondence*, 2:316.

30. Horace Walpole, *Walpoliana* (London: R. Phillips, 1799), 1:125–26.

31. Archibald S. Foord, *His Majesty's Opposition 1714–1830* (Oxford: Clarendon Press, 1964), p. 118.

32. Dickinson, *Bolingbroke*, p. 182.

33. This was Pulteney's claim in 1745, quoted by his chaplain, Thomas Newton, *Works* (London: John Francis & Charles Rivington, 1782), 1:40.

34. British Library, Additional MSS 18,915, fol. 29.

35. Dickinson, *Bolingbroke*, p. 194.

36. Ibid., p. 183.

37. There are considerable problems in attributing specific *Craftsman* essays to their various authors. It is certain that Amhurst, Bolingbroke, and Pulteney were regular contributors between 1726 and 1736. Amhurst continued as editor until his death in 1742. For a discussion of authorship, see Simon Varey, ed., *Contributions to the "Craftsman"* by Lord Bolingbroke (Oxford, 1982), introduction.

38. Dickinson, *Bolingbroke*, pp. 243–44, and William Cobbett, *Parliamentary History of England* (1811), 9:471–72.

39. So Bolingbroke wrote to Robert Knight, 12 June 1738; British Library, Additional MSS 34, 196, fol. 136^{r}.

40. *Boswell's Life of Johnson*, ed. George Birkbeck Hill, revised by L. F. Powell (Oxford: Clarendon Press, 1934–50), 1:268.

41. [Thomas Hayter], *An Essay on the Liberty of the Press* (London, [1754]), p. 28.

42. 20 February 1752, *The Letters of Philip Dormer Stanhope 4th Earl of Chesterfield*, ed. Bonamy Dobrée (London: Eyre & Spottiswoode, 1932), 5:1835.

43. ("Je perds un ami chaud, aimable, et instructif"), 30 December 1751, ibid., 5:1803.

44. To Swift, 25 March 1736; Pope, *Correspondence*, 4:6.

Chapter Two

1. John Locke, *Essay concerning Human Understanding*, ed. P. H. Nidditch (Oxford: Clarendon Press, 1975), bk. 3, chap. 10, pt. 34.

2. Richard I. Cook, *Jonathan Swift as a Tory Pamphleteer* (Seattle: University of Washington Press, 1967), p. 33.

3. Swift, *Gulliver's Travels*, ed. Herbert Davis (Oxford: Basil Blackwell, 1959), 4:5.

4. Alexander Pope, *Dunciad*, 4:23–26. This and all subsequent citations from Pope's poetry are taken from the Twickenham edition of Pope's poems, general editor John Butt, 11 vols. (London: Methuen, 1939–69).

5. To Pope, 18 February 1724; Pope, *Correspondence*, 2:220.

6. See, e.g., Dustin H. Griffin, *Alexander Pope: The Poet in the Poems* (Princeton: Princeton University Press, 1978).

7. *Craftsman* 130, 28 December 1728.

8. Cf. Cicero, *De Inventione*, the anonymous *Ad Herennium*, Quintilian, *Institutio Oratoria*, and George H. Nadel, "Philosophy of History before Historicism," *Studies in the Philosophy of History: Selected Essays from 'History and Theory,'* ed. George H. Nadel (New York, 1965), pp. 49–73.

9. *Examiner* 17, 30 November 1710; Swift, *The Examiner and Other Pieces Written in 1710–11*, ed. Herbert Davis (Oxford: Basil Blackwell, 1941, reprint ed., 1966), p. 26.

10. Joseph Spence, *Observations, Anecdotes, and Characters of Books and Men*, ed. J. M. Osborn (Oxford: Clarendon Press, 1966), 1:241.

11. "Pope and Bolingbroke on 'Examples': An Echo of the *Letters on History* in Pope's Correspondence," *Philological Quarterly* 52 (1973): 234.

12. Swift, *The History of the Four Last Years of the Queen*, ed. Herbert Davis (Oxford: Basil Blackwell, 1951, reprint ed., 1973), pp. 1–2.

13. *Intelligencer* 3; Swift, *Irish Tracts 1728–1733*, ed. Herbert Davis (Oxford: Basil Blackwell, 1955, reprint ed., 1970), p. 34.

14. Peter Dixon, *Rhetoric*, The Critical Idiom (London: Methuen, 1971), p. 53.

Chapter Three

1. Giles Barber, "Some Uncollected Authors XLI: Henry Saint John, Viscount Bolingbroke 1678–1751," *The Book Collector* 14 (1965): 531–32, lists all Bolingbroke's verse except "The Cloak: A Tale," *Craftsman* 249, 10 April 1731.

2. Swift, *Political Tracts 1713–1719*, ed. Herbert Davis and Irvin Ehrenpreis (Oxford: Basil Blackwell, 1953, reprint ed., 1973), p. 123.

3. For discussion of authorship of the *Examiner*, see J. A. Downie, *Robert Harley and the Press: Propaganda and Public Opinion in the Age of Swift and Defoe* (Cambridge, 1979), p. 127, and Swift, *Political Tracts 1713–1719*, pp. 123–24. A contemporary reader made the attribution for no. 6 on a copy now in the Bodleian Library, Hope fol. 17. Some notes of uncertain authority, written on copies in the British Library, Burney Collection vol. 148b, ascribe no. 8 to either Freind or St. John, no. 9 possibly to Freind, and no. 10 to Atterbury.

4. The *Letter* was later prefixed to editions of the *Examiner* in book form, and is now conveniently available in Swift, *The Examiner and Other Pieces Written in 1710–11*, pp. 221–27. Page references in parentheses after quotation refer to this text.

5. *A Letter from Monsieur Pett [ecu]m to Monsieur B[u]ys* (London, 1710). Pettecum and Buys were Dutch diplomats who had nothing to do with this publication. See Henry L. Snyder, "Daniel Defoe, Arthur Maynwaring, Robert Walpole, and Abel Boyer: Some Considerations of Authorship," *Huntington Library Quarterly* 33 (1969–70):133–53.

6. The principal poems in this convention (1665–67) are found conveniently in George deF. Lord, ed., *Anthology of Poems on Affairs of State: Augustan Satirical Verse, 1660–1714* (New Haven: Yale University Press, 1975), pp. 19–100.

7. John Dolben was a leading Whig M.P. who had first moved the disastrous impeachment of the Tory preacher Dr. Henry Sacheverell. Dolben had died on 29 May 1710. "Volpone" was a nickname for the earl of Godolphin, head of the previous government. Bolingbroke's gibe at Walpole is apparently his first in print.

8. *Examiner* 50, 26 July 1711.

9. Downie, *Robert Harley and the Press*, pp. 181–82.

10. *The Representation of the Right Honourable the Lord Viscount Bolingbroke* (1715), p. 5. Page references in parentheses after quotation refer to this text.

11. Swift, *Political Tracts 1711–1713*, p. 57.

12. Anon., *Cicero's Second Oration against Catiline, applied to the Present Times* (London, 1715), p. 4.

13. At least six different versions of this letter were printed in April 1715. Barber lists five, and the Huntington Library posssesses a

sixth. George Granville, Baron Lansdowne, later opposed Bolingbroke's attainder and was himself imprisoned in September 1715 on suspicion of Jacobitism. The *Letter* is not always thought to be Bolingbroke's, as several contemporary writers noted. Two possible authors are Atterbury and Lansdowne himself.

14. One version, *The Case of the Right Honourable the Lord Viscount Bolingbroke* (London, 1715), adds a postscript.

15. Anon., *The Important Letter Relating to the Affairs of Great-Britain* (London, 1715), p. 17.

16. *Works*, 1:113. The *Letter* is printed in *Works*, 1:111–79. Page references in parentheses after quotation refer to this text.

17. Geoffrey Butler, *The Tory Tradition: Bolingbroke, Burke, Disraeli, Salisbury* (London: John Murray, 1914), p. 14.

18. Baratier, *Bolingbroke: Ses Ecrits Politiques* (n.p., 1939), p. 180, and Dickinson, *Bolingbroke*, p. 145.

19. "Philalethes," *Some Remarks on the Late Lord Bolingbroke's Famous Letter to Sir William Windham* (London, 1753), pp. 56, 58–59.

20. See letters to Swift, 17 March N.S. 1719 (Swift, *Correspondence*, 2:314–18), to Alary, 13 May N.S. 1721 (*Lettres Historiques, Politiques, Philosophiques et Particulières de Henri Saint-John*, ed. Philippe Henri Grimoard, Paris, 1808, 3:84), and to his father, 24 July 1717 (British Library, Additional MSS 34,196, fol. 2^{v}).

21. Swift, *Correspondence*, 2:414.

22. *Réflexions sur l'Exil, écrites en anglois par Mylord Bolingbroke* ([Berlin], 1752), preface, p. 3.

23. See *Beauties of Hume and Bolingbroke* (London, 1782), p. xviii; [Caleb Fleming], *An Apologetical View of the Moral and Religious Sentiments of the Late Right Honourable Lord Viscount Bolingbroke* (London, n.d.), p. 1; Baratier, *Bolingbroke*, p. 171.

24. *Lettres*, ed. Grimoard, 3:22.

25. Ibid., 3:163–64.

26. 13 July N.S., 1724; *Lettres*, ed. Grimoard, 3:193.

27. *Reflections concerning Innate Moral Principles* (London, 1752). The tract is supposedly a reprint of a French edition published in Paris "*since his Decease*" (p. 84), but I have not traced such an edition. The pamphlet is printed with parallel French and English texts: Bolingbroke apparently wrote it in French, and someone else translated, but my references (in parentheses after quotation) refer to the English text.

Chapter Four

1. Simon Varey, "The Publication of the Late *Craftsman*," *Library*, 5th series, 33 (1978):230–33. Quotations from the *Craftsman* in this chapter are taken from one of three sources: Bolingbroke's *Works*, vol. 1;

Contributions to the "Craftsman," ed. Simon Varey (Oxford, 1982), hereafter designated in parentheses in the text by V and a page number; or original issues in the British Library, Burney Collection. In each case the number and date of the original issue are given, and page references appear in parentheses after quotation.

2. Cholmondeley (Houghton) MSS, P74, fol. 7; Anon., *The Danverian History of the Affairs of Europe for the Year 1731* (London: J. Roberts, 1732), and Simon Varey, "*The Craftsman* 1726–1752: An Historical and Critical Account," Ph.D. dissertation, Cambridge University, 1976, chap. 2.

3. Ernest Renan, *Histoire du Peuple d'Israel* (Paris: Calmann Lévy, 1887–93), 1:105–6.

4. Acts 19:24–27. See also Deut. 27:14–15 and Hosea 13:2–3. Cf. Kramnick, *Bolingbroke*, p. 274.

5. Bertrand H. Bronson, "The Writer," in *Man vs. Society in Eighteenth Century Britain*, ed. James L. Clifford (Cambridge: Cambridge University Press, 1968), pp. 114–20.

6. J. H. Plumb, *Sir Robert Walpole: The King's Minister* (London: Cresset Press, 1960), p. 141.

7. *Works*, 1:203.

8. Ibid., 1:206–7.

9. Kramnick, *Bolingbroke*, p. 49.

10. The "Assientos" were the South Sea Company's trading concessions won by Britain from Spain as part of the Utrecht settlement in 1713. They were unprofitable to the point of farce and in any case were systematically dishonored by Spain. The company repeatedly complained, without success, to the British government about violation of the Assiento agreement (British Library, Additional MSS 25,560–61).

11. The others appeared in nos. 105, 130, 131, 133, and 134.

12. Varey, *Contributions to the "Craftsman,"* pp. 82–88. Johan de Witt was shot, and his brother Cornelius battered to death before their bodies were left to the disposition of a mob, which tore them to pieces.

13. Cited in *Dictionary of National Biography*, under Bambridge.

14. See *Works* 1:492–95.

15. This was also published separately in 1731. See David Green, *Blenheim Palace* (London: Country Life, 1951), p. 174.

16. To Swift, 2 August 1731; Swift, *Correspondence*, 3:490.

17. The whole series is printed in *Works* 1:292–455; hereafter page references are given in parentheses in the text.

18. See nos. 220 (19 September 1730); 221 (26 September 1730); and 224 (17 October 1730).

19. *Craftsman*, nos. 86, 87, 93, 95, 99, 136, 138, 141, and 153.

20. *Craftsman* (1737), 8:vi.

21. Swift to Pope, 12 May 1735; Swift, *Correspondence*, 4:334; Bolingbroke to Knight, British Library, Additional MSS 34,196, fol. 95.

22. *Works*, 2:5–6. The *Dissertation* is printed in *Works* 2:5–172; page references are given in parentheses in the text.

23. Kramnick, *Bolingbroke*, p. 26.

24. See above, p. 55.

25. *Works*, 1:496–508. Kramnick, *Bolingbroke*, p. 29.

26. *Craftsman*, nos. 346 (17 February 1733), 350 (17 March 1733), 351 (24 March 1733), and 353 (7 April 1733).

27. William Cobbett, *The Parliamentary History of England* (London, Longman, Hurst, et al., 1806–1820), 9:471–72.

Chapter Five

1. Baron Hyde (formerly Viscount Cornbury) to David Mallet, 7 March N.S. 1752, said that copies were destined for Pope, Wyndham, Bathurst, Marchmont, Murray, Lyttelton, and Bolingbroke himself (British Library, Additional MSS 4948A, fol. 438^{v}). But see George H. Nadel, "New Light on Bolingbroke's *Letters on History*," *Journal of the History of Ideas* 23 (1962):557. Pope probably printed, but did not circulate, a substantial number.

2. By 1755, two more editions, five translations, and at least thirteen responses (eleven of them hostile) had been published.

3. Isaac Kramnick, ed., *Historical Writings* by Lord Bolingbroke (Chicago, 1972), introduction, p. xxxii.

4. Ibid., p. xv.

5. 1 July N.S. 1719; *Lettres*, ed. Grimoard, 3:24.

6. To Alary, 12 April N.S. 1722; *Lettres*, ed. Grimoard, 3:162.

7. Hyde to Mallet, 7 March N.S. 1752; British Library, Additional MSS 4948A, fol. 438^{r}.

8. Pope, *Correspondence*, 2:249–52.

9. Pope's edition omits these extra two pieces. The eight letters can be found in *Works* 2:173–334; hereafter page references cited in parentheses in the text.

10. See Kramnick, *Historical Writings* by Lord Bolingbroke, introduction; Nadel, "New Light," and J. G. A. Pocock, *The Ancient Constitution and the Feudal Law* (Cambridge, 1957).

11. John Leland, *Reflections on the late Lord Bolingbroke's Letters on the Study and Use of History* (London, 1753), pp. 8–9.

12. Kramnick, *Historical Writings*, p. xxiv.

13. Ibid., p. xxxvi.

14. Robert Clayton, *A Vindication of the Histories of the Old and New Testament, in Answer to the Objections of the late Lord Bollingbroke* [*sic*] (Dublin, 1752), p. 52.

15. Ibid., p. 65.

16. G. M. Trevelyan, ed., *Bolingbroke's Defence of the Treaty of Utrecht* (Cambridge: Cambridge University Press, 1932). Nadel, "New Light," p. 557, argues that Bolingbroke "did not consider the last two letters to belong to the subject of his work": he may not have intended to publish all eight together, but they form a complementary work, part theory, part practice.

17. Pocock, *Ancient Constitution and the Feudal Law*, p. 246.

18. Leland, *Reflections*, pp. 155–56.

19. [Caleb Fleming], *An Apologetical View*, pp. 1–2.

20. Leland, *Reflections*, p. 159.

21. *Works*, 2:352. The *Letter* is printed on pp. 352–71; hereafter page references cited in parentheses in the text.

22. Kramnick, *Bolingbroke*, p. 80.

23. D. G. James, *The Life of Reason* (London, 1949), p. 196.

24. H. T. Dickinson, "Bolingbroke: 'The Idea of a Patriot King,'" *History Today* 20 (1970):13–19.

25. Giles Barber, "Bolingbroke, Pope and the *Patriot King*," *Library*, 5th series, 19 (1964):67–89, and Frank T. Smallwood, "Bolingbroke *vs.* Alexander Pope: The Publication of the *Patriot King*," *Papers of the Bibliographical Society of America* 65 (1971):225–41.

26. Cf. Herbert Butterfield, *The Statecraft of Machiavelli* (London, 1940), pp. 154–55, and J. H. Grainger, "The Deviations of Lord Bolingbroke," *Australian Journal of Politics and History* 15, no. 2 (1969):55.

27. Pope, *Epilogue to the Satires, Dialogue I*, 1:160.

28. Pope, *Dunciad*, 4:188.

29. Anon., *The Impostor Detected and Convicted* (London, 1749), p. 24.

Chapter Six

1. *A Letter to Sir William Windham, Some Reflections on the Present State of the Nation, A Letter to Mr Pope* (1753).

2. *Works*, 3:49. The philosophical writings are printed in volumes 3 and 4; hereafter page references appear in parentheses in the text after quotation.

3. Aware of the looseness of the term *deism*, I refer for a working definition of Bolingbroke's deism to Walter M. Merrill, *From Statesman to Philosopher: A Study in Bolingbroke's Deism* (New York, 1949), p. 17: "Bolingbroke's deism, like that of his contemporaries, is readily analyzable into two aspects—one positive, the other negative. The positive aspect consists of his theories of Providence, miracles, evil, immortality, and finally, natural religion and ethics. The negative aspect consists of

a criticism of metaphysics and theology and of revelation. To some extent both of these aspects of deism, and to a great extent the positive one, are based on a conception of God as a being infinitely powerful and wise and external to the world."

4. Dickinson, *Bolingbroke*, p. 302.

5. Cf. Maynard Mack, *The Garden and the City: Retirement and Politics in the Later Poetry of Pope 1731–1743* (Toronto: University of Toronto Press, 1969), pp. 161–62, who shows that Caroline can occasionally be identified as Queen Dulness in the *Dunciad*.

6. Pope, *Correspondence*, 2:351.

7. Hayter, *An Essay on the Liberty of the Press* (London, 1754), pp. 20–21.

8. John Hill, *Thoughts Concerning God and Nature* (London, 1755).

9. Ralph Heathcote, *A Sketch of Lord Bolingbroke's Philosophy* (London, 1755), advertisement.

10. George Anderson, *A Remonstrance against Lord Viscount Bolingbroke's Philosophical Religion* (Edinburgh, 1756), p. 3.

Chapter Seven

1. Kramnick, *Bolingbroke*, p. 219.

2. Edwin Graham, "John Gay's Second Series, the *Craftsman* in Fables," *Papers on Language and Literature* 5 (1969):17–25.

3. Sven Armens, *John Gay: Social Critic* (New York: King's Crown Press, 1954), p. 190; Kramnick, *Bolingbroke*, p. 307.

4. See Mack, *The Garden and the City*, passim.

5. Mabel H. Cable, "The Idea of a Patriot King in the Propaganda of the Opposition to Walpole, 1735–1739," *Philological Quarterly*, 18 (1939):127.

6. *Works*, 2:165.

7. E.g., Kramnick, *Bolingbroke*, p. 209.

8. *The Poems of Jonathan Swift*, ed. Harold Williams, 2d ed. (Oxford, 1958), 2:484, 530–36, and *Craftsman* 25 (3 March 1727), and 30 (20 March 1727). See above, pp. 36–38.

9. Pope, *Dunciad*, 4:604.

10. *Works*, 3:127.

11. Pope, *Dunciad*, 4:643–46.

12. *Works*, 2:13.

13. Professor Mack's findings, revealed at the 1977 conference of the American Society for Eighteenth Century Studies, are as yet unpublished.

14. The poem's anti-monarchic (and anti-George) tone was still identified even without these passages.

15. Louis Bredvold, "The Gloom of the Tory Satirists," in *Pope and His Contemporaries: Essays Presented to George Sherburn,* ed. James L. Clifford and Louis A. Landa (Oxford: Oxford University Press, 1949), p. 3.

16. Swift to Pope, 1 November 1734; Swift, *Correspondence*, 4:263; and Pope to Swift, 15 September 1734; Swift, *Correspondence*, 4:254.

17. For discussion of the possible influence of Bolingbroke's philosophical writing on the composition of the *Essay on Man*, see Maynard Mack's introduction to the poem (Twickenham edition, 3:i), pp. xxvi–xxxi, and Kramnick's rejoinder, *Bolingbroke*, p. 306.

18. Swift to Pope, 1 November 1734; Swift, *Correspondence*, 4:263–64; and Spence, *Anecdotes*, 1:127.

19. Swift to Pope, 12 May 1735; Swift, *Correspondence*, 4:335; and Spence, *Anecdotes*, 1:127.

20. Pope to Swift, 25 March 1736; Pope, *Correspondence*, 4:6.

21. James Hervey, *Remarks on Lord Bolingbroke's Letters on the Study and Use of History* (Dublin, [1752]), p. 33.

22. Hugh Blair, *Lectures on Rhetoric and Belles Lettres* (London and Edinburgh, 1783), 1:399–400 and 2:238–39.

23. Chesterfield to his son, 12 February 1754, *Letters*, 5:2081.

24. Chesterfield, 18 March 1751, *Letters*, 4:1700.

25. James Ralph, *A Critical History of the Administration of Sr Robert Walpole* (1743), p. 346, and *Times* (London) *Literary Supplement*, 16 August 1923.

Selected Bibliography

This list can be supplemented by Giles Barber's checklist of Bolingbroke's works, "Some Uncollected Authors XLI: Henry Saint John, Viscount Bolingbroke, 1678–1751," *Book Collector* 14 (1965):528–37. Contemporary translations and reprints, listed by Barber, are not included here. Titles are listed in Section 3 below only if they are not printed in any of the collections or selections.

PRIMARY SOURCES

1. Collections

The Works of the late Right Honorable Henry St. John, Lord Viscount Bolingbroke. 5 vols. London, 1754. David Mallet's edition.

The Works of Lord Bolingbroke. 4 vols. London: Henry G. Bohn, 1844. Reprint. London: Frank Cass, 1967. Although not very well edited, and incomplete, this is the standard collection.

2. Selections

Contributions to the "Craftsman." Edited by Simon Varey. Oxford: Clarendon Press, 1982. Contains all of Bolingbroke's contributions other than those printed in the standard collection. An introduction discusses the problems of attribution.

The Craftsman. By Caleb D'Anvers [i.e., Nicholas Amhurst, Lord Bolingbroke, William Pulteney, et al.] 14 vols. London, 1731–37. This is a reprint of nearly all the articles from no. 1 to no. 511. The original folios are very scarce.

Historical Writings. Edited by Isaac Kramnick. Chicago: University Press, 1972. Although only a reprint of *Letters on the Study and Use of History* (omitting Letter 7 and part of Letter 8) and *Remarks on the History of England* (omitting the last letter), this volume has a useful short introduction.

3. Separate Prose Works

A Copy of My Lord Bolingbroke's Letter to My Lord—. London, 1715. The authenticity of this brief piece is still doubted.

A Familiar Epistle to the Most Impudent Man Living. London, 1749. Bolingbroke's undistinguished reply to Warburton over the *Patriot*

King controversy. It is conveniently reprinted, together with *A Letter to the Editor of the Letters on the Spirit of Patriotism, &c.* (1749) with an introduction by Donald T. Siebert, Jr., Augustan Reprint Society (Los Angeles: William Andrews Clark Memorial Library, UCLA, 1978).

A Letter to the Examiner. London, 1710. Printed as an appendix to Jonathan Swift, *The Examiner and Other Pieces Written in 1710–11*, edited by Herbert Davis (Oxford: Basil Blackwell, 1941, reprint ed. 1966), pp. 221–27.

Letter III. Of the Private Life of a Prince. 1740? Apparently a deleted portion of Pope's privately printed edition of the *Idea of a Patriot King*. A unique original is in the British Library.

Reflections Concerning Innate Moral Principles. Written in French by the late Lord Bolingbroke. And Translated into English. London, 1752. Printed in parallel texts.

The Representation of the Right Honourable the Lord Viscount Bolingbroke. London, 1715.

4. Correspondence

There is still no complete collection of Bolingbroke's correspondence. The most important printed collections of his letters are found in the volumes listed here.

The Correspondence of Alexander Pope. Edited by George Sherburn. 5 vols. Oxford: Clarendon Press, 1956.

The Correspondence of Jonathan Swift. Edited by Harold Williams. 5 vols. Oxford: Clarendon Press, 1963–65.

Letters and Correspondence, Public and Private, of Henry St. John, Viscount Bolingbroke, during the Time he was Secretary of State to Queen Anne. Edited by Gilbert Parke. 2 vols. London, 1798.

Lettres Historiques, Politiques, Philosophiques et Particulières de Henri Saint-John, Lord Vicomte Bolingbroke, depuis 1710 jusqu'en 1736. Edited by Philippe Henri de Grimoard. 3 vols. Paris: Dentu, 1808.

Lettres Inédites de Bolingbroke à Lord Stair 1716–1720. Edited by Paul Baratier. N.p., 1939.

SECONDARY SOURCES

Akstens, Thomas. "Pope and Bolingbroke on 'Examples': An Echo of the *Letters on History* in Pope's Correspondence." *Philological Quarterly* 52 (1973):232–38. Usefully links the exemplar view of history with Pope's view of satire.

Anderson, George. *A Remonstrance against Lord Viscount Bolingbroke's Philosophical Religion. Addressed to David Mallet, Esq; the Publisher*. Edinburgh, 1756. One of the more responsible protests against the philosophical writings, here considered to be erroneous, immoral, impious, and atheistic.

Baratier, Paul. *Bolingbroke: Ses Ecrits Politiques*. N.p., 1939. Oriented to biography rather than criticism, but still a fairly useful survey of Bolingbroke's political career.

Barber, Giles. "Bolingbroke, Pope and the *Patriot King*." *Library*, 5th series 19 (1964):67–89. An account of the mysterious publishing history of the *Idea of a Patriot King*. See also Smallwood, below.

Biddle, Sheila. *Bolingbroke and Harley*. New York: Alfred A. Knopf, 1974. A readable account of the feud during Harley's ministry, 1710–14, but Biddle reaches the same conclusions as Geoffrey Holmes in his much shorter study.

Brett, John. *Letters to his Grace the Lord Primate of all Ireland. Containing a Vindication of the Doctrine and Character of Saint Paul, in Answer to the Objections of the late Lord Bolinbroke* [*sic*]. Dublin, 1755. A routine denunciation of Bolingbroke's philosophy, but Brett is more interesting when he ventures uncertainly into the field of Bolingbroke's politics.

Briggs, E. R. "The Political Academies of France in the Early 18th Century; with Special Reference to the Clubs [*sic*] de l'Entresol, and to its Founder, the Abbé Pierre-Joseph Alary." Ph.D. dissertation, Cambridge University, 1931. The only attempt at a history of Alary's club since the Marquis d'Argenson's memoir (appended to Grimoard's edition of Bolingbroke's *Lettres*, vol. 3).

Butterfield, Herbert. *The Statecraft of Machiavelli*. London: G. Bell & Sons, 1940. Chapter 4 ("Machiavelli and Bolingbroke") is a hostile commentary on Bolingbroke's "turgid political writing," illustrating his large debt to Machiavelli.

Cable, Mabel Hessler. "The Idea of a Patriot King in the Propaganda of the Opposition to Walpole, 1735–1739." *Philological Quarterly* 18 (1939):119–31. Indicates the minor "opposition" literature inspired by Bolingbroke's *Idea of a Patriot King* and by his "patriotism" in general.

The Case of the Right Honourable the Lord Viscount Bolingbroke. London, 1715. An unusually sympathetic treatment of Bolingbroke's flight to France in 1715, this treatise also prints a postscript to *A Copy of a Letter from Dover*.

Cholmondeley (Houghton) Manuscripts. These are Walpole's private papers, deposited by the Marquess of Cholmondeley in the University Library, Cambridge. Of particular relevance to Bolingbroke are the documents (file P74) seized from the *Craftsman*'s printer on 3 September 1730.

Dickinson, H. T. *Bolingbroke*. London: Constable, 1970. Although not intended as a biography only, this is the only reliable and scholarly biography of Bolingbroke, but it also offers a coherent overall interpretation of his career and his writings.

———. "Bolingbroke: 'The Idea of a Patriot King.'" *History Today* 20 (1970):13–19. Reduces the *Idea* from its usual status as Bolingbroke's "best" work.

Downie, J. A. *Robert Harley and the Press: Propaganda and Public Opinion in the Age of Swift and Defoe*. Cambridge: Cambridge University Press, 1979. A useful account of the rise of the press during the ministry of Robert Harley. Downie thinks Harley much more influential than Bolingbroke on the development of the press, and illustrates very clearly the two men's divergent concepts of censorship and taxation of the press.

Fletcher, Dennis J. "Bolingbroke and the Diffusion of Newtonianism in France." *Studies on Voltaire and the Eighteenth Century* 53 (1967): 29–46. Argues for Bolingbroke's rôle as an "aggressive defender" of the Newtonian "faith."

———. "The Fortunes of Bolingbroke in France in the Eighteenth Century." *Studies on Voltaire and the Eighteenth Century* 47 (1966): 207–32. An interesting account of Bolingbroke's reputation as a writer in France.

Grainger, J. H. "The Deviations of Lord Bolingbroke." *Australian Journal of Politics and History* 15, no. 2 (August 1969):41–59. Not, as the title might suggest, about Bolingbroke's sexual activities, but a survey of his reputation, his style, and his place in British political literature.

Hanson, Laurence. *Government and the Press 1695–1763*. Oxford: Oxford University Press, 1936. The standard account of the law (usually libel) affecting printers of periodicals.

Hart, Jeffrey. *Viscount Bolingbroke, Tory Humanist*. Toronto: University of Toronto Press, and London: Routledge & Kegan Paul, 1965. Amid much error, borrowing, and vagueness, Hart includes a very interesting discussion of Machiavelli and Bolingbroke.

Hervey, James. *Remarks on Lord Bolingbroke's Letters on the Study and Use of History*. Dublin, [1752]. Not so much an attack on Bolingbroke as a defense of the Bible against his attack. Hervey was obviously not sympathetic to Bolingbroke, but he tried to be fair.

Hervey, John, Lord. *Some Materials towards Memoirs of the Reign of King George II*. Edited by Romney Sedgwick. 3 vols. London: Eyre & Spottiswoode, 1931. Fascinating and important insights into contemporary court and political life, recorded by one of the sharpest observers.

Holmes, Geoffrey, ed. *Britain after the Glorious Revolution 1689–1714*. London: Methuen, 1969. Two articles are especially valuable: A. D. MacLachlan, "The Road to Peace 1710–13," and the editor's "Harley, St. John, and the Death of the Tory Party."

Jackman, Sidney Wayne. *Man of Mercury: An Appreciation of the Mind of Henry St. John, Viscount Bolingbroke*. London: Pall Mall Press, 1965. A lively and entertaining analysis of Bolingbroke's philosophical writing.

James, D. G. *The Life of Reason: Hobbes, Locke, Bolingbroke*. London: Longman, Green & Co., 1949. One of the few systematic studies of Bolingbroke's philosophical works, this acknowledges the quality of his style while denying not only philosophical merit but even any philosophical conception.

Kramnick, Isaac. "An Augustan Reply to Locke: Bolingbroke on Natural Law and the Origin of Government." *Political Science Quarterly* 82 (1967):571–94.

———. *Bolingbroke and His Circle: The Politics of Nostalgia in the Age of Walpole*. Cambridge, Mass.: Harvard University Press, 1968. Demonstrates convincingly the consistency of Bolingbroke's political ideology, showing that he and his literary friends drew much of their political theory from James Harrington, and that Bolingbroke's was a consistently hostile reaction to the growth of financial capitalism.

Leland, John. *Reflections on the late Lord Bolingbroke's Letters on the Study and Use of History*. London, 1753. Leland, hostile to Bolingbroke's treatment of the Bible, wrote formidably searching and judicious criticism.

———. *A View of the Principal Deistical Writers*. 2 vols. London, 1754, and *A Supplement to the . . . View*, London, 1756. The first volume concentrates on the seventeenth century deists, the remaining two volumes mainly on the deism of Bolingbroke. Leland was not fond of the deists.

Mansfield, Harvey C. *Statemanship and Party Government: A Study of Burke and Bolingbroke*. Chicago: University of Chicago Press, 1965. An important analysis of the two statesmen as political thinkers.

Merrill, Walter McIntosh. *From Statesman to Philosopher: A Study in Bolingbroke's Deism*. New York: Philosophical Library, 1949. A commentary on the deistic tendency of Bolingbroke's philosophical works: Merrill has the advantage over his eighteenth-century predecessors by writing intelligibly.

Nadel, George H. "New Light on Bolingbroke's Letters on History." *Journal of the History of Ideas* 23 (1962):550–57. Principally a discussion of Pope's privately printed edition of *Letters on the Study and Use of History* (1738). Nadel makes several useful suggestions about the relation of that text to the "official" edition, about Mallet's rôle, and about Voltaire's response to the work.

———. "Philosophy of History before Historicism." In *Studies in the Philosophy of History: Selected Essays from 'History and Theory,'* " edited by George H. Nadel, pp. 49–73. New York: Harper & Row, 1965. A most valuable article, especially for its sketch of the use of the example.

Pocock, J. G. A. *The Ancient Constitution and the Feudal Law: A Study of English Historical Thought in the Seventeenth Century*. Cambridge: University Press, 1957. Essential background for Bolingbroke's political appeal to the theory of an ancient, immemorial constitution.

———. *Politics, Language and Time: Essays on Political Thought and History*. New York: Atheneum, 1971. One essay, "Machiavelli, Harrington and English Political Ideologies in the Eighteenth Century," sets out the context for an understanding of Bolingbroke's political ideology, and can be regarded as an introduction to Kramnick's full-length study (q.v.).

Rogers, Pat. "Swift and Bolingbroke on Faction." *Journal of British Studies* 9, no. 2 (May 1970):71–101. A lucid account of an important element of the political vocabulary of Swift and Bolingbroke.

Sichel, Walter. *Bolingbroke and His Times*. 2 vols. London: James Nisbet, 1901–2. This is a comprehensive biography of Bolingbroke, but Sichel allowed his imagination to get the better of his judgment, passing off a great deal of speculation and sheer guesswork as fact.

Smallwood, Frank T. "Bolingbroke *vs.* Alexander Pope: The Publication of the *Patriot King*." *Papers of the Bibliographical Society of America* 65 (1971):225–41. Another account of the publication history of the *Idea of a Patriot King*.

Warburton, William. *An Apology for the late Mr Pope; on Occasion of the Editor's Preface to . . . the Spirit of Patriotism*. London, 1749. Warburton's spirited attack on Mallet and Bolingbroke, in which he seeks to defend Pope against the charge of treachery (over the printing of the *Patriot King*) by proving that the poet acted honorably.

———. *A View of Lord Bolingbroke's Philosophy; In Four Letters to a Friend*. London, 1754–55. A massive, hostile dismemberment of Bolingbroke's philosophical writings.

Index

Akstens, Thomas, 18
Alary, Pierre Joseph, Abbé 8, 30–31
Amhurst, Nicholas, 34, 55
Anderson, George, 111
Anne, Queen of Great Britain and Ireland, 5–6, 21–22, 23, 27
Arbuthnot, John, 11
Aristotle, 105
Arnall, William, 65
Assientos, 124n10
Atterbury, Francis, Bishop of Rochester, 20
Austria and the Austrians, 24

Bacon, Francis, 105
Bambridge, Thomas, 50
Bible, 82–83
Blair, Hugh, 116
Bolingbroke, Henry St. John, 1st Viscount: created viscount, 4; early life, 1; early political career, 1–3; escape to France, 6, 25–26; forms opposition to Walpole, 9–11, 51; in France, 7–8, 12, 30, 75; literary relations, 112–17; marriages, 2, 8; part in Treaty of Utrecht, 5; reinstatement in England, 7–9; relations with Hanoverian Succession, 6–7; relations with Old Pretender, 7, 26; relations with the press, 4–5, 20, 23; reputation, 1, 13–14, 115–17; reputation as traitor, 16, 30; return to England (1744), 12; Secretary of State, 3, 5, 23; self-justification, 19, 23–24, 26, 28–29, 32, 60, 90; self-presentation, 66, 84, 89

WORKS:
Copy of My Lord Bolingbroke's Letter to My Lord—, A, 25
Craftsman, The, miscellaneous contributions to, 4, 10, 11–12, 16–17, *34–55*, *72–77*, 113
Dissertation upon Parties, A, 12, *61–72*, 75–76, 113, 116
Fragments, or Minutes of Essays, 107–11
Freeholder's Political Catechism, The, 75
Idea of a Patriot King, The, 13, 86, *98–101*, 112, 115
Letter on the Spirit of Patriotism, 12, *94–98*
Letter to Sir William Windham, A, 8, 16, *25–30*, 32
Letter to the Examiner, A, 4, *21–23*
Letters on the Study and Use of History, 12, 16, 18, 76, *78–94*, 102, 116
Letters, or Essays, addressed to Alexander Pope, 102–7
Occasional Writer, The, 11, 42
Philosophical Works: see *Letters, or Essays, addressed to Alexander Pope* and *Fragments, or Minutes of Essays*
poems, 20
Reflections Concerning Innate Moral Principles, 8, 31–32, 80

Reflections upon Exile, 30
Remarks on the History of England, 12, 18, 38, 49, *51–61*, 63, 68, 75, 76, 89, 113
Representation of the Right Honourable the Lord Viscount Bolingbroke, The, 24
State of Parties at the Accession of George I, 13, 26

Bredvold, Louis, 115
Brooke, Henry, 113
Bulkley, Charles, 111
Butler, Geoffrey, 26

Cable, Mabel H., 113
Caroline, Queen of Great Britain and Ireland, 68, 106
Catalonia and the Catalans, 24–25
Cato, 96
Charles Edward Stuart ('Young Pretender'), 99
Charles I, King of Great Britain and Ireland, 59, 63
Charles II, King of England, Scotland, and Ireland, 64, 66–67
Chesterfield, Philip Dormer Stanhope, 4th Earl of, 14, 116–17
Cicero, Marcus Tullius, 97, 106–107
Civicus (pseudonym), 43–45
Clarke, Samuel, 109
Clayton, Robert, Bishop of Clogher, 83
Cobham, Richard Temple, Viscount, 12
Colbert, Jean-Baptiste, 87
compassion, 31–32
Conduct of the Allies, The (Swift), 5, 23–24, 91
Consolatio ad Helviam (Seneca), 30
Constantine the Great, 41
constitution, 52–54, 56, 61–62, 67–68, 74, 75, 95, 99; of Spain, 64–65
Cornbury, Henry Hyde, Viscount, 12, 78, 90, 97
corruption, 17–18, 43, 45, 49, 50, 56, 59, 65–68, 81, 89, 93, 101
Craftsman The, 4, 10–11, 34–37, 52–53, 66, 72, 112; *see also* Bolingbroke: Works
Cudworth, Ralph, 108

Daily Courant, The, 51, 54, 57
D'Anvers, Caleb (pseudonym), *see Craftsman*
deism, 103, 126–27n3
Demosthenes, 97
Descartes, René, 105
Dickinson, H. T., 9, 10, 26, 98
Dixon, Peter, 19
Downie J. A., 23

elections (parliamentary), 47, 48, 56, 67, 75
Elizabeth I, Queen of England and Ireland, 58
Entresol, Club de l', 8, 30–31
Examiner, The, 4, 20, 22–23; *see also* Bolingbroke, Works: *A Letter to the Examiner*
examples, 17–18, 45, 49, 53–55, 56–57, 59, 62, 63–64, 73, 79–81, 83–85, 87–88, 95, 97; *see also* history
Excise Bill (1733), 10, 66, 73–74
exile, 30; *see also* Bolingbroke

faction, 52–54, 59, 62, 66, 100
'First Vision of Camilick, The,' *see* Bolingbroke, Works: *The Craftsman*
Fleming, Caleb, 89
Flying Post, The, 51, 55
Fog's Weekly Journal, 54

France and the French, 3, 12, 22, 24, 76, 78, 85, 87–89, 90
Francklin, Richard, 50, 51, 55–56, 58, 72–73
fraud, 45, 47; *see also* corruption
Frederick, Prince of Wales, 98–99
Free Briton, The, 65
Freeport, Charles (pseudonym), 45–47
Freind, John, 20

Garth, Samuel, 20
Gay, John, 1, 11, 112
George I, King of Great Britain and Ireland, 6, 10, 28, 60, 63
George II, King of Great Britain and Ireland, 55, 57–58, 63, 68–69, 76, 86, 96, 101, 114–15
Germany and the Germans, 24
Glover, Richard, 113
Godolphin, Sidney, 1st Earl of Godolphin, 2–3, 21, 60
government, 53, 69, 87, 93, 95; *see also* constitution, ministers, and Bolingbroke, Works: *A Dissertation upon Parties*
Guiscard, Antoine de, 4

Handel, George Frederick, 73, 74
Harley, Robert, Earl of Oxford, 2, 3, 4–6, 14, 23, 27
Hayter, Thomas, 111
Heathcote, Ralph, 111
Henry VIII, King of England and Ireland, 57–58
Hervey, James, 116
Hill, John, 111
history, 18, 31, 41, 51, 58–59; *see also* Bolingbroke, Works: *Letters on the Study and Use of History* and *Remarks on the History of England*
History of the Four Last Years of the Queen (Swift), 18
Hobbes, Thomas, 108
Homer, 105

irony, 17, 19, 39, 49–50, 52–53, 71

Jacobites and Jacobitism, 6, 7, 28–29, 30, 32–33, 36–37, 38, 53, 61
James, D. G., 97
James I, King of England, 59, 63
James II, King of England, Scotland, and Ireland, 89
James Edward Stuart ('Old Pretender'), 6, 7, 26, 27–29, 60, 73
Johnson, Samuel, 14
Juries Act (1730), 58

King, William, of Christ Church, Oxford, 20
Kramnick, Isaac, 5, 8, 73, 78, 97, 112

Lansdowne, George Granville, Baron, 25, 122–23n13
Leland, John, 79, 89, 93, 111
liberty, 42, 46, 52–54, 57–58, 59–60, 63, 66, 70, 75–76, 89, 96–99; of the press, 56–57, 72
Livy, 85
Locke John, 15
London Journal, The, 51, 54, 55, 56, 65
Lyttelton, George, 12

Mack, Maynard, 115
Mallet, David, 14, 102, 113
Mar, John Erskine, Earl of, 28
Marcilly, Marie Claire de (2nd Lady Bolingbroke), 8, 13, 30
Marlborough, John Churchill, Duke of, 2–3, 60
Maynwaring, Arthur, 21

Mazarin, Jules, Cardinal, 87
Medley, The, 22
ministers, 48, 50, 52, 62, 74, 95, 113
money, 40–42, 58, 68, 70–71, 81

Netherlands and the Dutch, 5, 22, 24, 87–88
newspapers, *see Craftsman, Daily Courant, Examiner, Flying Post, Fog's Weekly Journal, Free Briton, London Journal, Medley,* and prosecutions of printers, and Stamp Tax

Oldcastle, Humphrey (pseudonym), 51–52, 56
opera, 73
oratory, *see* rhetoric
Ormonde, James Butler, 2nd Duke of, 28

panegyric, 83–84
parliament, 1–4, 8, 10, 13–14, 38, 59, 67; *see also* elections
parties, political, 7, 13, 26, 90–91, 93; *see also* Bolingbroke, Works: *A Dissertation upon Parties,* Tories, and Whigs
patriot king, *see* Bolingbroke, Works: *The Idea of a Patriot King*
patriot opposition, 9–12, 95, 99, 112
Petticum, Mr. (pseudonym), 21
philosophy, natural, 102–104
piracy, 17
Pitt, James, 65
Pitt, William, 12
Plato, 103–105, 108
Plumb, J. H., 42
Pocock, J. G. A., 86, 94
Polwarth, Hugh, Viscount Polwarth, 12
Pope, Alexander, 1, 11, 12–16, 18, 68, 78, 98, 100–102, 105–106, 112–17
Pouilly, Jean Simon Lévesque de, 8
Pretender, Old, *see* James Edward Stuart
Pretender, Young, *see* Charles Edward Stuart
Prior, Matthew, 20
prosecutions of printers, 23, 42, 55–56, 58, 72
Protagoras, 108
Pulteney, William, Earl of Bath, 4, 9–10, 11, 13, 34, 37, 38, 60, 97
Pythagoras, 109

Randolph, Thomas, 111
revelation, 107–108
Revolution (1688), 42, 67, 81
rhetoric, 15–17, 23, 29, 32, 65, 69, 79–80, 88, 106–107
Richelieu, Alphonse Louis du Plessis de, Cardinal, 87
Rome, 53

satire, 18–19, 61, 83–84
Septennial Act, *see* elections
South Sea Company, 42–49, 70, 124n10
Spain and the Spanish, 24, 64–65, 87–88, 90–91; *see also* piracy, War of the Spanish Succession
Stamp Tax (1712), 23
stockjobbers and stockjobbing, 46, 48, 58, 70–71
Swift, Jonathan, 1, 4–5, 11, 13, 15–16, 18, 20, 23, 61, 114–17

Tacitus, 80, 84
Taylor, Brook, 8
Thomson, James, 113
Tories, 1–8, 9–10, 22, 26–27, 28–29, 38, 53, 66, 96

trade, 17, 42–49, 92; *see also* South Sea Company
Treaties: Pyrenean, 87; Seville, 51; Utrecht, 5, 24, 76, 83, 88, 93
Trevelyan, George Macaulay, 84
Turkey, 85

virtue, rhetorician's, 16–18, 19, 80, 94–95, 98, 113
Voltaire, François Marie Arouet de, 8

Walpole, Robert, 1st Earl of Oxford, 8–9, 10, 11–12, 14, 17, 18, 21, 23, 34, 36–38, 39, 41–42, 49–50, 52, 56, 59, 61–62, 63, 65, 66–72, 75, 76, 86, 88, 96–97, 114–15, 117
War of the Spanish Succession, 3, 5, 21, 26, 90–91
Warburton, William, 98, 111
West Indies, 36–37, 114
Whigs, 5–10, 12, 20–22, 26–27, 38, 53, 66, 90–92
William III, King of England, Scotland and Ireland, 89
Winchcombe, Frances (1st Lady Bolingbroke), 2, 13
Witt, Johan de, 49, 87–88, 124n12
Wyndham, William, 8, 9, 11, 13 32, 75, 97

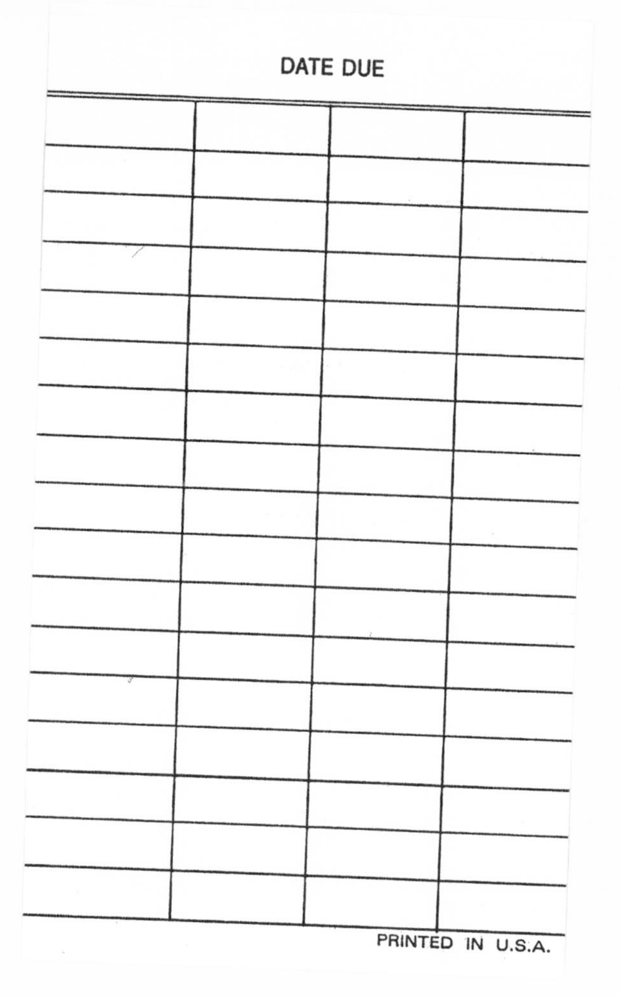
DATE DUE
PRINTED IN U.S.A.